KHAJURAHO

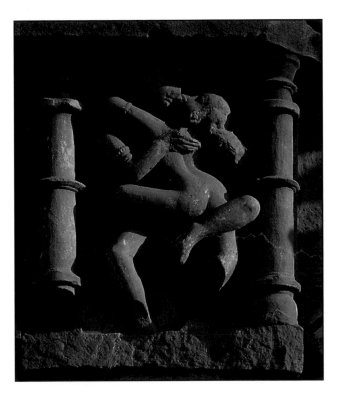

The temples of Khajuraho are renowned for their depiction of human passion in stone, and this is an example of the large body of erotica placed on the temple walls. This amorous couple is from a small niche facing north in a lower band of Vishvanath Temple. The woman's arms are twined about the man's neck like a garland, in a gesture of complete submission.

Acknowledgements

My grateful acknowledgemets go out to all our learned scholars (Mulk Raj Anand, Kanwarlal, Vidya Prakash, Krishna Deva and others), whose works have helped me in understanding some of the mysteries of Khajuraho; to friends of Khajuraho—writers and travellers from all over the world who have shared their experiences with me over two decade; to tourist guide Brijendra Singh; to my friend Kishore Singh, who had faith in my ability to write this book; to my children Ritika and Pragun, who actually goaded me into believing that I was not being presumptuous in doing so; to my husband Kanti and his brothers whose idealism and commitment towards the development of Khajuraho proved very infectious; and finally, my respects to my late father-in-law, Shyam Poddar, who was the emerging force behind all of us involved in the emergence of Khajuraho as an important tourist destination.

The photographer wishes to thank D.N. Dube who, as a friend, initiated and trained him in the art of creative photography; Brijendra Singh who was always at hand in Khajuraho and proved invaluable as a source of information; the Chandela Hotel for hospitality; and the drivers and guides of Khajuraho who provided affectionate assistance.

© **Lustre Press Pvt. Ltd., 1995**
M 75 GK Part II (Market)
New Delhi 110 048, India

ISBN: 81-7437-026-9

Text: Pramila Poddar (© Lustre Press), *Photographs:* Pramod Kapoor, *Photocredits (for pictures other than those of Pramod Kapoor);* Karoki Lewis (pages 16, 17, 33, 68-69, 73, 84, 86, 87, 91); D.N. Dube (pages 62, 71); Avinash Pasricha (page 90); Archaeological Survey of India (photographs of Adinath, Chaturbhuj, Devi Jagdamba, Duladeo, Vamana and Vishwanath temples on pages 92, 93 and 96); *Introduction, captions and text of pages 17, 32-51, 62 and 90;* Kishore Singh. *Text Editor:* Lakshmi R. Iyer. *Typesetting:* Fleming George P. *Artist:* Sudhir Peter.

Printed and bound at
Star Standard Industries Pte. Ltd., Singapore

KHAJURAHO
❖ *Temples of Love* ❖

Text
Pramila Poddar

Photographs
Pramod Kapoor

Lustre Press
Delhi ◇ Banaras ◇ Agra ◇ Jaipur ◇ The Netherlands

Genealogical Table
The Chandela kings who ruled over Khajuraho

Nannuk	(ruling c. A.D. 831)
Vakpati	(c. A.D. 831-850)
Vijaishakti	(c. A.D. 850-900)
Rahil	(c. A.D. 880-900)
Harshdev	(c. A.D. 900-925)
Yashovarman	(c. A.D. 925-954)
Dhang	(c. A.D. 954-1002)
Gand	(c. A.D. 1002-1018)
Vidyadhar	(c. A.D. 1018-1029)
Vaijpa	(c. A.D. l029-1050)
Devvarman	(c. A.D. 1051-1060)
Kirtivarman	(c. A.D. 1060-1100)
Sallakshanvarman	(c. A.D. 1100-1115)
Jaivarman	(c. A.D. 1115-1120)
Prithvivarman	(c. A.D. 1120-1129)
Madanvarman	(c. A.D. 1129-1163)
Yashovarman II	(c. A.D. 1163-1165)
Parmadidev	(c. A.D. 1165-1202)
Trailokyavarman	(c. A.D. 1205-1247)
Virvarman	(c. A.D. 1247-1287)
Bhojvarman	(c. A.D. 1288-1289)
Hammirvarman	(c. A.D. 1289-1308)
Virvarman II	(ruling c. A.D. 1315)

Contents

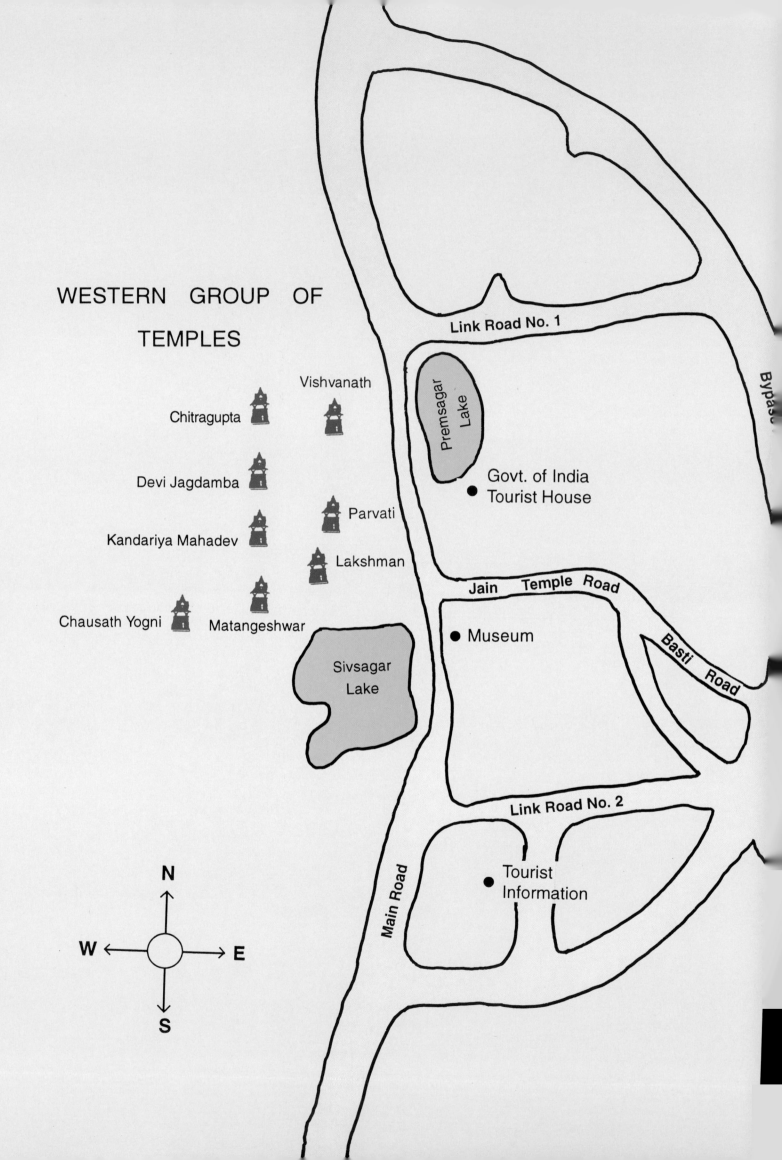

KHAJURAHO

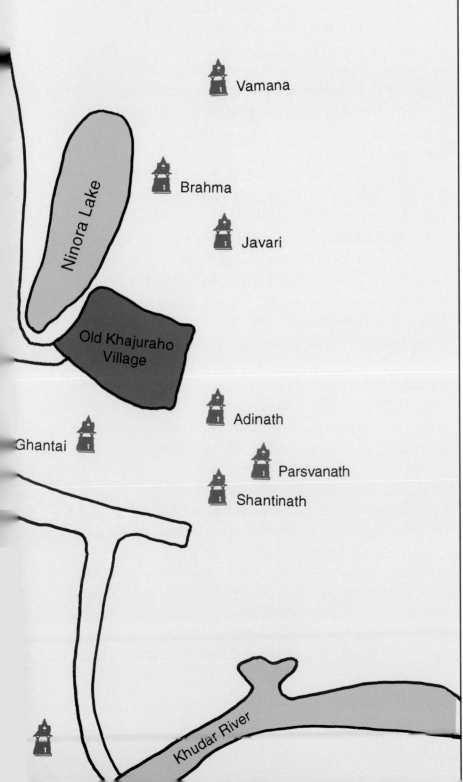

EASTERN GROUP OF TEMPLES

Vamana

Brahma

Javari

Ninora Lake

Old Khajuraho Village

Ghantai

Adinath

Parsvanath

Shantinath

Khudar River

Introduction

The village of Khajuraho is like a million other villages in India; what sets it apart is its medieval legacy of temples that represent the perfect fusion of architecture and sculpture.

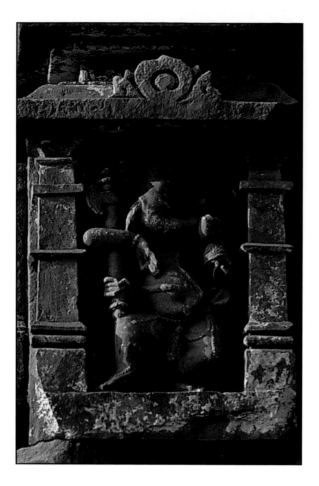

This Dancing Ganesh from a small niche in Vishvanath Temple highlights some of the popular attributes of Shiva's son. Ganesh is regarded as a remover of obstacles and is propitiated before other gods for this reason. This pot-bellied, elephant-headed god is sometimes shown in the role of his father, as a mendicant or as cosmic dancer.

LOCATED IN THE PROVINCIAL STATE OF MADHYA Pradesh, Khajuraho is known the world over for its temple architecture and sculpture. The construction of these thousand-year old temples took a little over two centuries; in terms of architecture, they form the high point of the north Indian 'nagara' style. Of the 85 temples believed to have been built between the 9th and 12th centuries only 20 have survived, many in splendid condition, others having given way to the ravages of time and nature.

Close to and around Khajuraho is forest land; a small clearing houses a village populated by no more than 3,000 residents, but visited each year by tourists from all over the world. Hotels, restaurants and souvenir shops front the entrances to the two distinctive groups of temples; little boys switch from Spanish to French to German in rapid succession as they peddle handicrafts or mineral water; signboards, too, are posted in various languages, and the villagers now seldom bother to look up when they hear the drone of aeroplanes overhead.

The focal point of tourist activity is, of course, the temples built by the Chandela Rajputs, who traced their descent from the Moon god. The head of the clan is reputed to have been a valiant warrior who fought lions bare-handed (hence the emblem, frequently seen at the temples, of a warrior grappling with a lion); he is said to have ordered the building of the temples as a means of salvation for his mother, Hemvati, who was ravished by the Moon god. The spate of temple-building which began about the middle of the 9th century and continued until the early 12th century must have used the services of thousands of sculptors, architects and masons; unfortunately, there is almost no record of this activity in the annals of Indian history. By the time the last temple was completed the Chandela dynasty had sunk into oblivion.

Khajuraho was the Chandela capital for only a brief period; they ruled for the most part from Kalinjar and other parts of the Bundelkhand region, with Khajuraho remaining their religious centre. The most important aspect of the temples is the abundance of sculptures that decorate the façades and interiors of the shrines. In this profusion of images attention has understandably been paid to divinities, less understandably to celestial beauties and the female form in general and, controversially, to graphic sexual representations. Over the years a number of explanations have been forthcoming for the presence of erotic sculptures at what was essentially a religious centre; no single theory, however, has been able to justify their profusion. Were these temples centres of tantrism, which cites sex as an important component of human development towards the Absolute — or were they merely a reactionary swing away from the austerities preached by the Buddha? Perhaps the answer will be found as excavations in the region continue, but this much is certain: Buddhism did at one time have a strong presence here, just as tantric rituals enjoyed a wide appeal during the medieval period.

As Chandela power diminished, the importance of their sometime-capital also waned. Its heavily forested terrain could not provide much revenue, and served to deter invading Muslim armies (for whom the temples were of little interest, while the sculptures could only have appeared offensive—they certainly did to T. S. Burt, the British engineer who is credited with their 'discovery' in the mid-19th century). The temples were never, strictly speaking, 'lost', for villagers and tribal inhabitants of the region were familiar with them; they continued to use one temple in particular — Matangeshwar Mahadev — for worship, especially on the occasion of Shivratri. While early travellers such as Alberuni and Ibn Batuta had reported the presence of the temples, they were not dwelt on at any length, possibly because of their being abandoned and overgrown by bushes and weeds.

Burt announced their presence to the world, and the first major data on them was collected by General Alexander Cunningham in his *Survey of India* reports. Early this century there was some interest in the temples, but their inaccessibility made their study and regular travel to the site impossible. Over time roads were laid and the minimal facilities provided; then, a couple of decades ago, the first luxury hotel project revived interest in the region, and the resurrection of Khajuraho began.

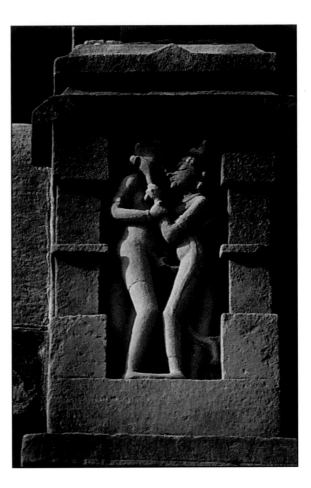

Facing north-east, below the traditional bands of sculpture, this small niche in Kandariya Mahadev Temple contains an amorous couple. The sculptor has taken liberties with their portrayal, endowing the piece with an underlying sense of humour; the woman pulls the man's beard while he makes love to her.

History
and Legend

The Chandela kings who ordered the building of Khajuraho's magnificent temples left no records of their life and times, or of their reasons for building these temples. Any theories about their major preoccupations must therefore be drawn from their sculptural legacy alone.

This frieze from the south-east wall of Lakshman Temple has a chieftain of the Chandela clan being entertained by soldiers with musical instruments. That he is attended by women shows him to be of high rank.

13

Subjects of everyday life have been adroitly dealt with in the friezes around the temples. This panel depicts the sculptors going about their task, chiselling an elephant from a block of stone: from the north-east platform of Lakshman Temple.

KHAJURAHO EXERCISES THE MIND, FIRES THE imagination. Hundreds of miles from civilization, deep in the hinterlands of central India where the tiger still has its domain and where the shadows of the forests hold their own secrets is a small clearing. Here: a village, modest by any standards; a tank, ambitiously called a lake; groups of ancient temples, some in ruins.

For most people, Khajuraho continues to remain an enigma, a question mark in the arena of world-art. What is the significance of its temples? What pattern did they fit into in the ancient past, and why were temples used as an art gallery? If there was a kingdom here, where are the remains of grand mansions and grander palaces? Why is it that only temples have been discovered? Were these temples religious in nature? If so, how does one justify the presence of some of the most graphic representations of sexual scenes the world has ever known? Art historians have tried for years to seek a solution to the mystery of Khajuraho, but all attempts to do so must eventually be reduced to conjecture, for there are no records to reveal the purpose for the building of these temples. Perhaps we will never know; what is certain, however, is that Khajuraho will continue to draw homage from travellers and art-lovers, as it has done ever since its revival.

An Ancient Past

Ancient dynasties are often shrouded in a veil of mystery, largely because written records are rare and, as is often the case in India, myth and legend weave their way over time into the history of their origin and their reign. And when the dynasty leaves a legacy as contradictory as the Khajuraho temples, with their mix of the religious and the sensuous, the web is woven of brighter threads, the accompanying legends more colourful.

Khajuraho or 'Khajur-vahika' (bearer of date-palms), also known as 'Khajjurpura' in ancient times, evidently derives its name from the golden date palms (khajur) that adorned its city gates and, if the varied legendary versions are to be believed, owes its existence to an enchanting maiden named Hemvati.

According to the account of the medieval court poet, Chandbardai, in the Mahoba-khand of his *Prithviraj*

Raso, Hemvati was the beautiful daughter of Hemraj, the royal priest of Kashi (Varanasi). One summer night, while she was bathing in the sparkling waters of a lotus-filled pond, the Moon god was so awestruck by her beauty that he descended to earth in human form and ravished her. The distressed Hemvati, who was unfortunately a child-widow, threatened to curse the god for ruining her life and reputation. To make amends for his folly the Moon god promised that she would become the mother of a valiant son. 'Take him to Khajjurpura', he is believed to have said. 'He will be a great king and build numerous temples surrounded by lakes and gardens. He will also perform a *yagya* (religious ceremony) through which your sin will be washed away.' Following his instructions, Hemvati left her home to give birth to her son in a tiny village. The child, Chandravarman, was as lustrous as his father, brave and strong. By the time he was 16 years old he could kill tigers or lions with his bare hands. Delighted by his feats, Hemvati invoked the Moon god, who presented their son with a touchstone which could turn iron into gold, and installed him as king at Khajuraho.

Chandravarman achieved a series of brilliant victories and built a mighty fortress at Kalinjar. At his mother's request he began the building of 85 glorious temples with lakes and gardens at Khajuraho and performed the *bhandya-yagya* which expunged her of her guilt.

A variation of the same legend introduces Hemvati as the widowed daughter of Mani Ram, the royal priest of Kalinjar. As a result of a mistake in his calculations the priest informed his king that a particular night was Puranmasi (full moon night) and not the dark night that it actually turned out to be. In her concern for her father's reputation the beautiful Hemvati prayed to the Moon god, who was gracious enough to uphold the word of the priest but, in return for his favour, ravished the daughter. The grieving father was so shame-stricken that he cursed himself and turned into a stone, which was later worshipped by the Chandelas as Maniya Dev. Hemvati gave birth to a son, the sage Chandrateya, who became the progenitor of the Chandela clan.

Historically speaking, the area around Khajuraho has always been renowned for its cultural achievements.

Inscriptions from Vishvanath Temple glorify the Chandela rulers and describe the attributes and prayers dedicated to the deities within. The inscriptions are in Sanskrit, the root Indian language, in the Devanagiri script which is still in use.

15

Shivratri Mela

ONE THEORY ABOUT THE KHAJURAHO temples surmises that the original 85 temples were built to commemorate the marriage of Shiva and Parvati. Shiva is the God of Destruction and part of the Hindu trinity, the source of regeneration which led to the worship of the phallus; his union with Parvati is regarded as the base of cosmic energy. This may explain some of the erotic figures on the temple walls as celebrating the powerful, divine union. The theory postulates that the sculptures were images of people captured in motion at the point when Shiva's marriage party arrived at the celestial town where the couple were to wed.

Certainly the underlying force of the temples is the worship of Shiva and Shakti, with a large number of images dedicated to this mendicant god surrounded by other divinities of the Hindu pantheon, celestial beings and humans in a drama of unending life.

Shivratri, the annual occasion celebrating the birth of Shiva, is a major Indian festivity, and the only one to be celebrated with traditional zeal at Khajuraho. It is the one link that has endured between Khajuraho past and present. Even when the temples were abandoned to the jungle, the temple bells would peal on Shivratri, as people from outlying areas came to this arena of the gods to pray before Shiva.

The date for Shivratri is calculated according to the Hindu solar calendar, and usually falls in March. Early that morning villagers arrive at Matangeshwar Temple to bathe the Shivling, the god's powerful phallic symbol, with milk and water. Fruits and flowers are offered to the deity, oil lamps lit and foreheads smeared with the *tilak*, while over the throng of people that will continue from dawn to late in the night, the temple bells peal as they must have done a thousand years before.

A procession of Shiva and Parvati images is taken through the village and the wedding takes place with complete rituals. A local *mela* (fair) springs up around the water tank where the people bathe before entering Shiva's presence. Here are folk acrobats, gymnasts, performers and sellers of the little wooden and clay toys that village children love.

Opposite page: *Shivratri Mela in February-March is the only local celebration associated with the temples in Khajuraho. The only temple in active use, Matangeshwar, is the focus of activities, thronged by devotees from dawn to midnight. Matangeshwar remained the venue for this annual festivity even when the temples were 'lost' to the world.*

Above: *As with most temples in India, the presence of a priest is essential to conduct the rituals associated with Hindu prayer and worship.*

17

Preceding pages: *The small Varaha Temple located close to Lakshman is dedicated to the boar incarnation of Vishnu. The large image of the boar in turn bears an estimated 67 images of divinities, celestial beings, demons and humans.*

This page: *The Chandela lion placed in the small Mahadev Temple shrine positioned between the Kandariya Mahadev and Devi Jagdamba temples. Since the progenitor of the Chandela dynasty was known to have fought barehanded with lions in his youth, the image of a warrior grappling with a lion has become the accepted emblem or monogram of the Chandela dynasty.*

One finds references to Kalinjar and Chitrakoot, which form part of this region, in the epics and the Puranas. Up to circa 400 BC it formed part of the Vatsa kingdom; in circa 200 BC it witnessed a remarkable flowering of sculpture and architecture during the Sunga period and, later, during Gupta times. In the 7th century the Chinese traveller Huien Tsang came across a number of Buddhist monasteries in Khaju-raho. Fresh excavations are revealing more evidence of the region's importance in Indian history. Nevertheless, it was the Chandela Rajputs who endowed it with its unrivalled cultural and political status.

Who then were the Chandelas, when not ruled by the myth of Hemvati and her heavenly paramour? The dynasty is grouped with the 35 Rajput clans of India who trace descent from the sun, the moon or the sacred fire. It would appear that the first Chandela chiefs were feudatories or subordinates of the Pratihara rulers of western India. As the power of the latter declined, the Chandela chief, Yashovarman (also known as Lakshavarman), successfully fought against the Rashtrakutas of south India and the Palas of east-ern

India and proclaimed himself an independent king. He led military expeditions towards the north and the south and took control of the mighty fortress at Kalinjar; under his regime the Chandelas became a power to reckon with. Yashovarman ordered the mag-nificent Lakshman temple and with this began the era of temple building that a thousand years later remains unrivalled in the realm of religious art. His successors Dhangdev, Ganda and Vidyadhar continued the brilliant building traditions of their predecessor.

It was during the reign of Vidyadhar, the most powerful of all the Chandelas, that Mahmud of Ghazni started his invasions of northern India. While Vidyadhar twice engaged Mahmud in battle, his successors could not withstand the continuous onslaught of the Muslims and their supremacy in the region declined. Although they continued to rule over a small territory comprising Mahoba, Kalinjar and Khajuraho up to the first quarter of the 14th century, from the end of the 11th century onwards they were considered only a minor northern Indian dynasty. The heyday of their glory was undoubtedly the period between 950-1050 AD, and it was during this period of comparative peace and prosperity that the greatest temples of Khajuraho were erected.

It is fortunate that though the later Chandelas were defeated a number of times by the Turks (both Mahmud of Ghazni and Mohammed Ghori), the temples did not suffer at the hands of the invaders. Probably the timely shifting of the capital to Kalinjar saved them from the wreck of invading fury. It is also possible that the Muslim armies never actually penetrated into Khajuraho, deterred by hills and dense jungles, rugged territory and a hostile populace. But the very factors which saved them from destruction became in turn responsible for the obscurity of these splendid temples, and for centuries these treasures remained sunk in oblivion, lost to the outside world. Of the original 85 temples, 20 have survived the ravages of time to proclaim the artistic reputation of the Chandelas and to immortalize the reign of their dynasty.

This small frieze placed below the large sculptures on the south wall of Vishvanath Temple depicts soldiers in combat. The large number of panels devoted to scenes of war mirror the social conditions of the time and the tasks of kingship before the Chandela rulers.

Sculpture

The sculptures that adorn the temple façades and interiors focus on the world of divinity, of women, and of mankind: their portrayal bridges the twin realms of the real and the ideal.

This south-facing lower band from Parsvanath Temple has an exquisite statue of an often-repeated Khajuraho subject: an apsara painting her eyes with kohl. She is flanked by the mythical shardul, a traditional combination of a horse and lion, on the left, and a rather more unusual one of a horse and elephant on the right. These, in turn, are flanked by images of Balram (Lord Krishna's older brother) and his consort, Revati, on the left, and of Lakshmi and Vishnu on the right.

23

The artisan would sometimes combine the attributes of Shiva and Vishnu in a single figure known as Hari Hara, such as this one from the Museum. The sculptor has given the combination of the two gods one body, but their hairstyles, ornaments and hand-held instruments distinguish the two; Shiva is shown with his trident, Vishnu with his discus.

THE FIRST IMPRESSION OF A KHAJURAHO TEMPLE IS that of one giant carving reaching out to the skies. A closer look, which brings into focus the hundreds of sculptures of gods and goddesses, celestial beauties and their enchanting human counterparts, mythical animals and the mundane, only serves to strengthen this impact. In the temples of Khajuraho architecture and sculpture are perfectly integrated, making them dual masterpieces of these arts.

The sculptures belong to the surface on which they are carved, as its constituent, integral part. They are not added from the outside after completion of the framework, but are carved out of the same blocks of stone which form the structural fabric of the temple. The builders evolved a formula for the placement of the sculptures, each set occupying its assigned zone, and this has been uniformly adhered to. Thus the temple rose, tier upon tier, with the sculptured slabs being placed simultaneously according to their scheme of depiction.

The region around Khajuraho was famous for its sophisticated stone art, as a wide variety of stone for assorted techniques of chiselling was available and the artisans had acquired extraordinary skills over the ages. Khajuraho itself is surrounded by hills forming offshoots of the Panna range which belong, in turn, to the Vindhyas. To its south, the river Ken (ancient Karnavati) and its tributaries have cut deep gorges through the massive Vindhyan sandstone. The upper Vindhyan or Kaimur stone provides excellent building material in the form of a fine-grained sandstone of rich shades, varying from buff to light pink, large quantities of which have been used for the temples.

Although it is based on classical traditions, the sculptural art of Khajuraho is essentially medieval. Situated in the heart of central India, it was open to the artistic influences of the east and west; it is this artful blending of the sensuousness of the east with the nervous angular modelling of the west that lends the sculptures of Khajuraho their amazing human vitality. The fine profiles, three-quarter profiles and back-views exhibit the sculptors' fascination with the human form. Judiciously placed along the recesses and protuberances, the sculptures mingle with the shadows which change their texture and effect from dawn to dusk in countless moments and moods.

The sculptural treasures created at the behest of the Chandela rulers can be divided into seven categories:

The cult images in the sanctum

The first category contains the cult images of Shiva, Vishnu, Surya, the Jain Tirthankaras, and so on, installed in the sanctum for worship. These are carved in strict accordance with the canons and injunctions laid down for the purpose, with their prescribed form and figure, bearing specific weapons and symbols and accompanied by their secondary deities. The largest sanctum image is that of the Dakshinmurti Shiva in the Chaturbhuj temple.

Other gods, goddesses and divinities

Hindu mythology in all its richness and variety finds expression on the walls of the Khajuraho temples. There are all the gods and goddesses of the Hindu pantheon: Brahma, Vishnu and Shiva, depicted with their spouses and in their various incarnations and forms. There are demi-gods, *dipkals* (regents of the quarters), *vidyadhars* (angels) attending the gods and *gandharvas* (celestial musicians). There are the powerful dwarf *ganas* (cherubs) and the *kumaras* (load-bearing, four-armed dwarfs) supporting structures with uplifted hands. Together with the celestial beauties, they create the illusion of heaven. The figures in the niches remain formal, like the cult images, but those sculptured on the walls are less so. In fact, they can only be distinguished from the human figures by their peculiar headdress, their mounts or special attributes, a suggestion of the diamond on the chest or a long necklace. In most cases, the gods dress as the humans do.

Apsaras, sura-sundaris and nayikas

The next class consists of the *apsaras* (celestial dancers), *sura-sundaris* (celestial beauties) and *nayikas* (beautiful women). The *apsaras* and *sura-sundaris* exist as the entertainers of the gods. These

The Hindu pantheon of gods and goddesses derives from the trinity which forms the principal cosmic force of evolution, consisting of Brahma the Creator, Vishnu the Preserver and Shiva the Destroyer. In this south-facing decorated niche in the upper band of Chitragupta Temple, Brahma is depicted with his consort, Saraswati. The temple also has similar images of Shiva, facing west, and Vishnu, facing north.

Overleaf: *These panels from the south-west wall of Duladeo Temple pay homage to Shiva in a number of sculptures depicting his most accepted form with his consort Parvati. The figure on the left in the middle panel is that of Vashu or Nandi, Shiva's mount, while Yama is positioned just below; Yama is the God of Death. The upper band consists of floating celestial beings known as gandharvas.*

celestial nymphs and their earthly counterparts, the *nayikas*, all blessed with grace, youth, beauty and charm, form an extremely important and really attractive element of the sculptural decoration at Khajuraho. As heavenly dancers, they are shown in intricate dancing poses; as attendants of higher divinities, they carry the lotus flower, ornaments and the like as offerings. Portraying different moods and emotions, these beauties can be seen rinsing water from their hair, removing a thorn, writing a letter, singing, playing the flute or decorating themselves in various ways. Free from any iconographical compulsions, they are pure and simple works of art *par excellence*. In hundreds of beautiful figures, forms and postures, they appear on the interiors of brackets and niches in the *mandaps*, in the circumambulatory and, on a much larger scale and with greater emphasis, around the exterior—each on her own pedestal and with irresistible individual appeal.

Sculptures depicting secular themes

Friezes and stray pieces of sculpture pertaining to secular themes cover different subjects like domestic life, groups of teachers and disciples, dancers and musicians, scenes of rituals and ceremonies and so forth. These provide an interesting insight into the lifestyle and society of medieval India. The *sutradhar* (architect) and *shilpin* (sculptor or artisan) are frequently depicted. On the *jagati* (platform) of the Lakshman temple, the master architect can be seen teaching a group of disciples; in the Vishvanath he supervises the temple-building, resting his chin and bent body on a wooden staff. Yet another frieze shows a piece being sculpted with hammer and chisels and then transported on a pole by six carriers. Wrestlers, acrobats, gladiators and hunters are graphically represented. Scenes of music and dance are common, with musicians generally being male; singers and dancers, female. Attendants carry bags slung from their shoulders and princes ride horses with footmen holding umbrellas over them. A couple is seen in serious discussion; another entertains a group of friends. One mother tempts her child with a bunch of mangoes, another takes her infant from the lap of a servant. There are also numerous scenes of the army

Top: *A large sculpture of Shiva from a north-facing wall on a subsidiary shrine of Lakshman Temple.*

Above: *A seated Shiva from the west-facing upper band of Duladeo Temple.*

The back wall of Devi Jagdamba Temple, facing west, has as its principal characters the Hindu trinity, depicted in a somewhat unusual manner. The figure in the lower band is that of Vamana, the dwarf incarnation of Vishnu; the central band has Shiva in his Mrityunjaya (one who has conquered death) manifestation; the upper band, Brahma with his consort Savitri.

on the march and processions marked by gaiety and revelry.

Sculptures of natural and mythical animals

These include some remarkable representations of real and mythical animals. Of special interest are the *shardul*, the lion, the cosmic boar and the rat. Elephants are shown in combat and in a playful mood, one pulling the leg of the other with its trunk. Camels, though rare, can be seen on the Vishvanath temple. The *shardul*, a fabulous beast, is a popular theme at Khajuraho and has rich symbolic significance. It is always a combination of two animals, with the lower half mainly that of a horse, while the upper part could be a horned lion, elephant, boar or even a peacock.

Mithuns

Then there are the *mithuns*, the erotic couples or groups which, strictly speaking, belong to the category of secular themes. Friezes on some lower panels, often accompanying scenes of armies on the march, depict bestiality. Further up are single sculptures of women, courting couples and amorous ones, totally absorbed in themselves, in various erotic poses. Some of these capture the fine nuances of human emotions; a lover presents a gift to his beloved but makes her first cover her eyes; another mischievously encourages a monkey in order to draw his nervous companion closer. The serene expressions of the participants are in striking contrast to the physical abandon and acrobatic postures of some figures. In the recesses occur some orgiastic scenes involving complicated poses, often explained as tantric rituals and practices.

There are different theories regarding the fluid bends and curves shown by some figures to a seemingly impossible degree. While some scholars attribute these to yoga and calisthenics, others suggest that the artisan gave full vent to his imagination, going even further than was prescribed by the *Kamashastra*. A highly convincing theory is one which claims that these so-called 'picture-positions' on the walls were due to the constructional needs of the temple which required that the images be placed on a vertical axis, even if they were conceived and carved in a lying-down position. Visualized horizontally arranged, many of these compositions, with their tortuous and difficult poses, immediately shed all their mystery.

The temples built in the prosperous days of the Chandela dynasty, such as the Lakshman, Parsvanath, Devi Jagdamba and Kandariya Mahadev, display manifold variations on the erotic theme, while the later ones like the Chaturbhuj and the Adinath are less erotically oriented. In the Duladeo, the erotic element is totally absent. Though the erotic sculptures of Khajuraho have received the maximum exposure, they form only a part of an entire range of carvings.

Geometrical bands and floral motifs

In addition to these categories are the beautiful sculptural bands which adorn the outer and inner wall surfaces of the temples and the ornate motifs on the pillars and ceilings inside the temples, which exhibit intricate workmanship. The *ardh-mandap* ceiling of the Lakshman temple is considered one of the best in central India.

This page: *Vishnu in his realm: an impressive sculpture of the Preserver as depicted within a bracket in the upper band of the north wall of Devi Jagdamba Temple.*

Overleaf: *Shiva in his aspect as Bhairav is recognized by the familiar attributes of a trident and a snake though his mount, the bull Nandi, has been replaced by a dog. This bracketed figure is from Lakshman Temple.*

Page 31: *A Jain mother goddess, Vidya Devi, similar to the Hindu goddess of learning, Saraswati. Both are depicted with the veena (a stringed musical instrument), books, a lotus and a pot. This bracketed image is from the lower band of Parsvanath Temple's south-facing wall.*

This page: *A beautiful study of a celestial nymph from the Museum, depicting the Indian ideal of feminine beauty: full, rounded breasts, a slim waist and curvaceous hips. This figure also highlights the large eyes, aquiline nose and generous lips that mark an Indian beauty.*

Facing page: *Though the temples of Khajuraho (with the exception of Matangeshwar) are no longer used for religious purposes, this statue of Parvati from the inner sanctum of Devi Jagdamba Temple has the devout paying homage to her for she, with her consort Shiva, is Shakti, the source of primordial energy. This was not the original figure in the sanctum, but the replacement dates back to the same period as the temples.*

A Study of the Masterpieces

On a first visit the temples of Khajuraho are overwhelming, for the mind is hard put to grasp the wealth of sculptures, the strict adherence to an architectural pattern and the integration of the two into a whole. To be able to identify the best representations of sculptural art in Khajuraho, visitors should specifically seek out the following specimens in different categories as among the finest representations of Indian sculptural art.

Gods and Goddesses: The very best sculptures in this category would include the following:

DURGA, LAKSHMAN TEMPLE. This sculpture, fully intact, glorifies the many-armed goddess; her countenance is blissful.

VISHNU, CHATURBHUJ TEMPLE. Of the many Vishnu images in Khajuraho, this is easily the best for the balance with which the facial expressions, ornamentation and anatomical details are represented.

ARDHNARISHWAR, CHATURBHUJ TEMPLE. Shiva and Parvati as Ardhnarishwar, half man-half woman, is the key concept of Khajuraho, and expresses the fusion of energy in consciousness.

SHIVA-PARVATI, KANDARIYA MAHADEV TEMPLE. Parvati is seated on Shiva's left thigh, and the divinities are gazing into each other's eyes.

GANGA-YAMUNA, LAKSHMAN TEMPLE. The two river-goddesses at the entrance to the sanctum are carved in very fine detail and convey a feeling of controlled movement. The same images housed within the Museum are also very good representations.

PARVATI, MUSEUM. A sculpture that would rank among the finest in the country for the balance with which the figure has been sculpted; no part of the body has escaped the scupltor's meticulous chisel.

Celestial Nymphs: These sculptures of dancers, singers and musicians depict the woman as entertainer, portraying the unconscious erotic appeal of a woman's body movements.

From the Lakshman Temple, the following specific celestial nymphs draw attention: woman writing a letter; woman playing a flute; woman putting *sindoor* (vermilion powder on forehead and parting of the hair indicating that she is married); woman yawning and

Mythical Figures

Top: *Kirtimukha, often called the lion-mask motif in Indian art, is found with great frequency in Khajuraho, usually as a decorative frieze that runs as a band before the lower panel of sculptures, and often between different bands. This frieze is from Lakshman Temple.*

Above: *A typical shardul figure from the circumambulatory passage of Lakshman Temple facing the north balcony. The shardul is a mythical beast, half horse, half lion, that portrays the struggle between knowledge and wisdom depicted by the two human figures always associated with it.*

KHAJURAHO'S TEMPLE SCULPTURES HAVE quite a number of depictions of mythical beings, often not the main figures in the bands of sculpture that adorn the temples, but playing the role assigned to them by myth and in the hands of the sculptors.

Shardul: The most commonly found sculptures, interspersed freely among the *apsaras* or celestial beauties, are figures of the *shardul,* traditionally an imaginatory creature which represents the animal within mankind. In its most common depiction it is seen with two miniaturised figures of men, one riding on its back, the other placed by its feet. While the figure on the back symbolises ignorance, with the *shardul* attempting to swallow it, the one below represents knowledge. The *shardul* depicts the constant battle between knowledge and ignorance, between good and bad, especially with regard to the human emotions portrayed on the temple walls ranging from passion to ego, jealousy and lust, all seen as human weaknesses. The image of the *shardul* is therefore a cautionary note for those visitors who see only what is offered to them by society and religion, bypassing the responsibility without which indulgence in human passions cannot be overcome.

Traditionally depicted as a combination of a horse and a lion, the *shardul* is also, in some cases, shown as a combination of a horse and an elephant or peacock, camel or parrot, and, very unusually, a horse's body with the head of a man. These variations are unique to Khajuraho.

Keechak: Keechak is the figure usually placed atop a column which takes upon itself the weight of the temple walls, of the *shikhars* and balconies. Keechak is identified in Indian mythology as a dwarf wrestler of immense strength who served in the court of King Virat, the ruler in whose empire the five Pandava brothers and their bride, Draupadi, found sanctuary during the exile imposed on them by the Kauravas. Since they were supposed to be incognito, Keechak tried to take liberties with Draupadi, and was killed by Bhim. He has, however, endured as a symbol of strength, so strong that he could lift elephants with his stunted hands, placing them over his shoulders. He was, therefore, the perfect figure to be used in the decorative idiom, carrying the burden of the temples.

The dwarf is usually blessed with a great deal of strength in Indian myths, and is often shown as an attendant figure for royalty or nobility. It was during the Sunga and Kushan periods that the dwarf began to find identification on the platform of Indian art.

Kirtimukha: Used primarily as a decorative motif in friezes, Kirtimukha finds a place in Indian mythology as an evil demon who pleased Lord Shiva with years of worship. Lord Shiva was forced to ask him what he wanted as a boon. The demon asked for something to eat that would never finish, and Shiva granted him the boon, with the condition that he would have to eat himself. The demon had no choice but to obey, and the world was thereby rid of the evil monster. Kirtimukha is usually depicted with a face akin to a dragon's and something in its mouth, at the end of which is another small face, signifying self-annihilation.

Keechak, the load-bearing dwarf, is placed on top of columns to take on the weight of the temple walls and spires. This mythical figure of great strength is believed to have been a wrestler in the court of King Virat as mentioned in the great Indian epic, the Mahabharata. The placement of the apsaras by his side is part of the grand design, but the couple above the window is an example of the kind of surprises Khajuraho has in store for the observer willing to look beyond the obvious.

35

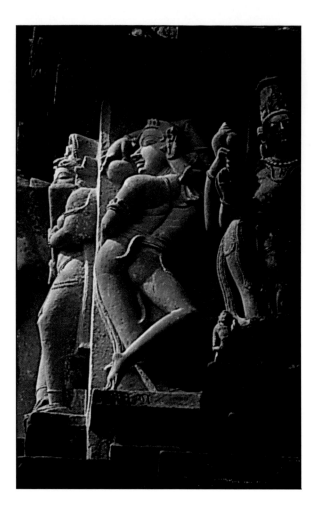

Preceding pages: *Agni, the Fire God, with his consort Swaha, from the north-facing middle band, Parsvanath Temple. Images such as these, with the male divinity placing one hand lightly beneath the bosom of his consort, depict the oneness of being, the sublimity of union and the transference of human lust to a higher plane.*

This page: *The Lakshman Temple wall facing south has a surfeit of apsara figures, and those in the upper band are particularly exquisite in their detail. Among these, the oft-repeated figure of a woman playing with a ball reaches a high level of artistic excellence. The apsaras on this band sport elaborate coiffures, each different from the other.*

stretching her back; woman showing a letter with an attitude of supplication.

From the Kandariya Mahadev Temple, the following examples of the celestial entertainer should be viewed: woman removing her lower garments to reveal her genitalia, with a scorpion on her thigh representing passion; woman pouring wine into the cup held in the hands of a man; woman with a bunch of mangoes and a parrot; a woman standing lost in thought while a monkey tugs at her clothes; the stylised pose of a woman dressed in the fashion of the age.

From the Devi Jagdamba Temple: a woman offering her body in total submission to a man; putting *sindoor* on her forehead; woman showing the wrinkles on her genitalia, again with a scorpion on her thigh; woman pulling the beard of a man.

From Vishvanath Temple: look out for the *nayikas*, known for their lissom figures and sharply-defined features, at variance with similar figures in the other temples. Note the hairstyles, ornaments and the highly developed clothes-sense. The figures look like they have been specially posed, and are very elegant.

Vamana Temple: two studies of posed figures of celestial nymphs that are renowned for their beauty and detail.

From Parsvanath Temple: Studies of nymphs in various poses, for example, while applying collyrium to the eyes, painting the feet with *alta*, painting a wall, removing a thorn from the foots, tying ankle bells preparatory to a dance performance.

From Adinath Temple: a dancer in the typical pose of the area, with a drummer seated by her feet; applying *sindoor* on her forehead; note the detail with which they have been captured in stone.

From Duladeo Temple: one figure is most striking, that of a nymph tying a waist belt.

Two other categories of celestial beings must be mentioned here. The first consists of *gandharvas* (nymphs in the floating position holding flower garlands), *kinnaras* (celestial musicians) and *vidyadhars* (holding swords). The best examples of these are to be found on the upper bands of the Parsvanath and Duladeo temples. The other category consists of the *shalbhanjikas* or tree-goddesses and there are two fine sculptures of these in the *maha-mandap* of the Lakshman temple, while the *maha mandap* of the Kandariya Mahadev temple has one very fine specimen. In addition, the Museum has three *shalbhanjikas* that merit attention.

Mithuns or Erotic Couples: There are two bodies of sexual representation in sculpture on the temple walls. The first deals with the amorous pairing of gods and goddesses, primarily Shiva-Parvati and Vishnu-Lakshmi, as well as some amorous couples on the upper bands representing sex as a bond, creating oneness, and depicting *moksha*. The more explicit sculptures reveal the lust essential to sexual intercourse, over which humans must rise to levels of sublimity. While there is a reasonably large body of erotics, not all of them manage to convey the pleasure of sexual union through facial expressions and through anatomical and ornamental detail. The best erotics are the following:

Lakshman Temple: facing south, a large sculpture of a couple kissing, the body of the woman pressed against the man's; to the north-west, in a small bracket, an amorous couple with passion evident not only on their faces but in the movement of their bodies as well; and to the north-east, a touch of the humorous in a frieze that shows an elephant next to a couple, laughing as it watches them make love.

In the Lakshman temple, which has the largest number of erotic sculptures, a frieze outside the temple platform and small friezes around the main temple and inner sanctum contain orgiastic scenes and display naked lust, with the spirituality of sex missing.

Chitragupta Temple: contains a beautiful depiction of a kiss, with the woman offering her body in total submission to the man.

Kandariya Mahadev: has few erotics, though it is regarded as the finest temple in Khajuraho for its attention to architectural detail. Its best-known erotic sculpture suggests a yogic posture, with the figure of the man upside down, supported by two female assistants who are part of the orgiastic scene. According to some, the figure shows signs of tantric influences.

Devi Jagdamba Temple: has the finest amorous

The Kandariya Mahadev Temple is architecturally the most superior in Khajuraho, but with the attention to architectural detail, the sculptures have remained secondary and are therefore rarely exceptional. These figures from the north wall, facing east, must be individually appreciated: one supplicating with a letter, the other lost in thought, with a monkey tugging at her dress.

Khajuraho's Nymphs

A MAJOR HIGHLIGHT OF THE sculptures at Khajuraho has been the depiction of apsaras in their moments of leisure, captured forever in stone images, but kept alive through a play of light and shadows. Many images depict them at their toilette or at tasks that are not strenous, representing instead the idleness of the upper echelons of society in medieval times.

1. On a wall from Devi Jagdamba Temple, an apsara plays with a ball.
2. This apsara is probably a dancer, shown placing a belt around her waist. The ornaments she wears are carefully detailed. From the west-facing lower band on the north wall of Duladeo.
3. Facing north, this lower band from Vishvanath Temple has a woman squeezing out water from her hair after her bath. Note the elegant anatomical details, the flower blossoms in her hair and the jewellery she wears.
4. The woman putting vermilion on her forehead is a subject that is often repeated at Khajuraho; this sculpture is from the north wall of Devi Jagdamba Temple.
5. A nymph concentrates on applying henna to her hand in the portion that has been added to the rear of Parsvanath Temple.

1

2

3

4

5

6

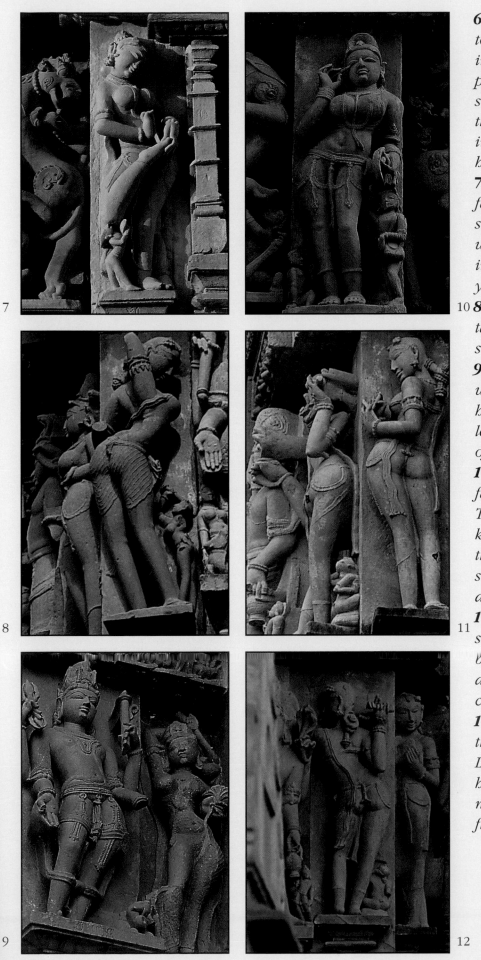

7

8

9

11

12

6. *The lower band of the north wall to the rear of Lakshman Temple is important for the figure of a woman pulling out a thorn from her foot. A small attendant supports her foot in this task; what is of particular interest is the handbag slung from his shoulder in contemporary style.*

7. *This panel from the lower south-facing band of Parsvanath Temple shows a woman painting her feet with* alta, *a tradition still prevalent in parts of India, especially among young brides and dancers.*

10 **8.** *A celestial nymph attends to her task of writing a letter: a frequent study at Khajuraho.*

9. *An apsara appears lost in thought while disrobing, half her dress having fallen away to display one leg. From the south-west-facing wall of Vamana.*

10. *A sculpture from the south-facing lower band of Parsvanath Temple shows a woman applying kohl to her eyes. This is one of only three or four sculptures on the subject, and is probably the best among them.*

11. *A beautiful representation of the sensuousness that the sculptor has brought to bear on the images of apsaras, such as this one of a celestial nymph scratching her back.*

12 . *An apsara playing the flute from the east-facing lower band of a Lakshman Temple north wall. Note her elaborate hairstyle, and the movement of her fingers on the flute.*

The middle band from the Lakshman Temple, facing south, has this famous kissing couple—one of the finest examples of erotic art, especially with regard to the fluid langour of the body postures. The band also has a number of naagkanyas (female images with crowns of serpents). The central figure of Vishnu is flanked by a singer and an apsara applying vermilion to her forehead.

couples in sculpture in Khajuraho. Three couples here are truly outstanding in the field of sculptural art, located respectively facing south, south-west and east.

Vishvanath Temple: two sculptures, one facing south, the other west, merit particular attention for the unusual poses of the couples making love—acrobatic and physically impossible, they are representative, nevertheless, of the artistry of Khajuraho's sculptors.

Mythical Figures: Some of the fine mythical figures depicted here are found nowhere else outside of Khajuraho. The *shardul* figure dominates sculptural art in Khajuraho. An unusual *shardul* sculpture in Lakshman temple shows this mythical creature dominated by man. Other unique *shardvls* with varying expressions include three sculptures in Parsvanath Temple and two in Adinath Temple. The finest Keechak figures include two of these dwarf load-bearers at Lakshman Temple, their expressions depicted very clearly. The Lakshman Temple also has the best depiction of Kiritimukhas in a frieze.

Dwarfs: The figure of the dwarf has been used to fill in space, and specific roles. A study must be made of the dwarf holding the *kalash* next to the figure of Ganga in the Museum. The Lakshman temple has a frieze of elephants with dwarfs in between. In the Jain temples of the Eastern Group they assume the role of attendants. Individual sculptures of dwarfs can be seen in the Museum.

Battle Scenes: Though these panels are not large, they convey a good idea of the activity that went into waging war during the medieval ages, ranging from actual battles to the marching of armies, soldiers in combat and entertainment off the battlefield. These scenes are best depicted in the friezes of the Lakshman, Vishvanath and Kandariya Mahadev temples.

Everyday Life: These scenes are important for an understanding of the social and economic mores of the age. The Lakshman temple shows artists chiselling stone, pilgrims, dancers, musicians, schools and more. The Vishvanath temple has religious processions, dancers, musicians, helpers from the army and such like. Isolated panels can also be studied in the Museum.

Inner Sanctum Figures: Some of the figures in the inner sanctum are outstanding examples of the art of stone sculpture as practised in the medieval ages. Those that specifically draw attention include the Vaikuntha or multi-headed Vishnu in the Lakshman temple, the Parvati sculpture in the form of Shakti in the Devi Jagdamba temple, the Shivling phallic representation of Shiva in Vishvanath and Matangeshwar temples, the Dakshinmurti representation of Shiva at Chaturbhuj temple, and the Suryamurti or statue of the Sun God in Chitragupta temple. Also of interest is the sanctum of Parsvanath temple with its original sculptures surrounding the more recent one of the Jain Tirthankara.

Lesser Seen Sculptures

On a brief visit one is rarely likely to have the opportunity of discovering the hidden wealth of Khajuraho's sculptures. At the same time, it is worth the effort to keep one's eyes open to look beyond the obvious. Some of the best sculptures are to be seen on

This page: *This damaged figure is a brilliant study of lovers kissing, the expressions on their faces depicted very clearly. From the lower, south-west facing band of Chitragupta Temple.*

Overleaf: *This is a sculpture that is very easily overlooked by many visitors to Devi Jagdamba Temple. Located on the east-facing wall close to the entrance portico, it reveals an intimacy between the lovers arising from an understanding that goes beyond mere desire.*

the façades and within the temples. These can be independently observed, or a guide will single out those which are outstanding examples because of their subject matter.

For those who wish to see beyond what is on immediate offer, here are some pointers to the discovery of sculptures not commonly viewed.

The very best examples of sculptural art are usually to be found in the depiction of *apsaras* or celestial nymphs. Often, some of the best of these are located at eye level within the *mandap* or the ambulatory of the main temple. Though the light in the temples is never bright, it is sufficient to study the sculptures, especially to read their expressions and note the fine details with which they have been invested. As an example, the Lakshman Temple has a sculpture of an *apsara* holding a letter in one hand, with some writing visible on the letter; she holds up two fingers of her other hand and has a beseeching look on her face. This masterpiece is rarely viewed by most visitors. What the *apsara* is attempting to do is show viewers

Top left: *An interesting sculpture from the north-facing middle band of Devi Jagdamba Temple. The couple seem to be sharing an intimate moment; the woman plays with the beads in the man's necklace. Is there some hidden anxiety she is attempting to convey through her silence?*

Top right: *This amorous couple from the north wall of Devi Jagdamba Temple's upper band is an outstanding example of the oneness of man and woman in their quest of the sublime. The intertwined bodies appear as one, while the man's eyes seem to indicate that he has entered a trance.*

the letter with her lover's village mentioned on it, and requesting them to carry her letter to him over a journey only two hours long.

Some images of gods and goddesses are placed far above eye level, and visitors must make an effort to stand at the edge of temple platforms and survey the upper reaches of the temples to spot some masterpieces — for instance, the beautiful depiction of Lord Ram with a bow and arrow in the Lakshman temple; or Agni, the fire god, in minute detail. The higher end of the Vishvanath temple has a sculpture of Vishnu in his universal form as recounted in the epic *Bhagvad Gita.* Again, there are some very good examples of divinities to be seen at the highest levels of the ambulatories, difficult to spot because of the very soft natural light filtering in through the windows. The Lakshman temple has the complete *Krishna Leela* depicted along the upper end of the circumambulatory; this often escapes attention as well.

Some of the best hidden' sculptures deal with erotics. One should spend time looking for these in the small friezes along the temple walls, especially as part of the war scenes. These small sculptures also frequently display a remarkable sense of humour. Here are orgies, scenes of sexual perversion and more. Within the circumambulatory of the Lakshman temple, if one were to look at the lowest band of minute sculptures along the floor (you may have to lie down to see some of these), there are some rarely-viewed scenes of sexual perversion, especially relating to the woman being made love to by an assortment of animals ranging from the tiger to the wild boar. Above the balconies along the façade of the Vishvanath temple (you will have to stand at the far edge of the platform to try to see these) is a profusion of erotic sculptures that is easily missed because it is not at eye-level.

Animal Sculptures

Khajuraho is the domain of woman in her varied expressions, but her male counterpart has not been ignored on the canvas of the sculptured walls. The male divinity and the male consort both lend a semblance of balance to the profusion of female images. Along with these, there is some depiction of scenes of battle and everyday life, and it is here that the largest number of animal figures have been shown.

The friezes depict elephants on the march; the elephant is singled out for particular representation. In a historical and religious context, the elephant has always been closely associated with the Indian psyche; at Khajuraho, its body contours are perfectly chiselled whatever its activity, whether on the march, in battle or as part of a procession. The artist has frequently taken the liberty of endowing it with a sense of humour and other endearing human characteristics. During a march, one elephant tries to trip another before it, while elsewhere a laughing elephant shares the erotic exploits of a couple.

The treatment of the horse is pragmatic, without the fine detail attendant to the elephant sculptures, for the Chandelas were not equestrian warriors, though the army did have its cavalry. The horse is often used in examples of bestiality, and to depict the *shardul*, the mythical beast whose lower half resembles that of a

The west wall of the south-west corner of Devi Jagdamba Temple has this delightful portrayal of a sophisticated couple out for a walk. The sculpture is notable for the facial expressions, the display of ornaments and hairstyles and the fluid movements of the human body.

Friezes of Animals

T HE SMALL BANDS that girdle temple walls but are not devoted to the principal sculptures often combine men in battle or at their daily tasks with those of animals, particularly the elephant. These are delight- 1 fully representative of a society in which animals played a major role and formed a significant component of the human drama.

1. A battle scene from the north platform of Lakshman Temple depicts the use of elephants in combat. Elephants formed an important component of medieval Indian armies, and were specially trained for warfare.

2. In this frieze of elephants from the south platform of Lakshman Temple, their contours and movements have been wonderfully captured in stone. The artisan has risen above the ordinary by investing them with character, particularly in the depiction of one elephant trying to trip another directly ahead of it.

2

3

3. The elephant sculptures at Khajuraho possess endearing human qualities; this frieze from the west-facing north wall of Lakshman Temple shows an elephant adjacent to a couple making love, laughing at them in a warm sharing of their intimacy.

4. This study of camels from the battle friezes of the south-facing platform wall of Lakshman Temple is of interest because camels form a very rare component of the animal sculptures at Khajuraho.

4

5. A delightful sculpture from Kandariya Mahadev Temple has a hunter on horseback attacking a lion with his sword. The more usual depiction of the lion was in the Chandela monogram with a large lion shown grappling with a warrior

5

6. This frieze from a panel adorning the south platform of the Lakshman Temple depicts animal passion in humans in the form of bestiality. Though the horse forms part of the Chandela army as depicted on the temple platforms and façades, it is rarely given the detailed treatment reserved for elephants.

6

49

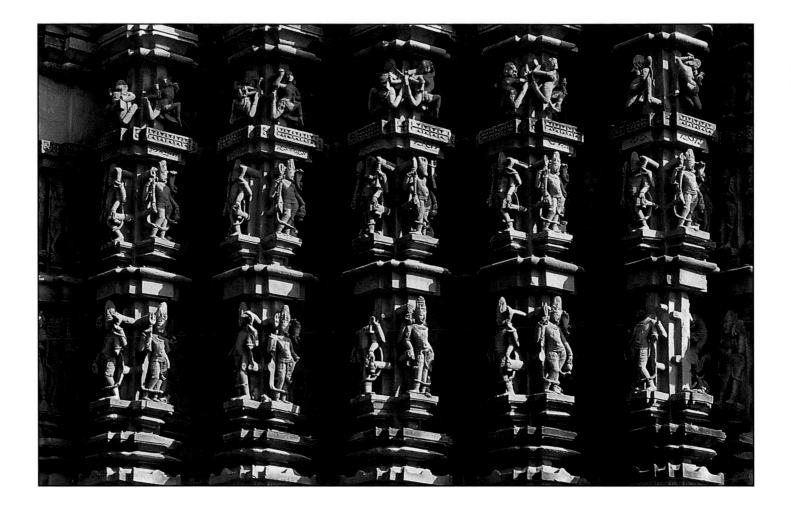

Duladeo Temple has a very large number of Shiva sculptures, perhaps more than any other temple. These bands on the south-west part of the temple consist of flying gandharvas on the upper band while the middle and lower bands have Shiva sculptures and those of his mount, Vashu.

horse. Sculptures of the camel are few and far between; it had little use in the heavily forested environs of the Chandela kingdom.

The monkey is used as a prop in the principal bands of sculpture, usually in roles which highlight its mischievous nature. It is depicted pulling at a woman's dress, or disturbing an amorous couple. The parrot is usually seen with a woman and child, or a woman carrying bunches of fruit.

The overriding large sculpture is that of the lion, independently placed before the temples on platforms in front of the subsidiary shrines. The figure of a warrior grappling with it appears towards its front. This is considered to be the image of a Chandela king, possibly the first, who had earned himself a reputation for being able to take on a lion bare-handed. This sculpture, repeated often and without variation, is seen as the emblem or monogram of the Chandela dynasty.

Scenes of nature, of trees, flowers and shrubs are so rare as to be non-existent; it would seem that the

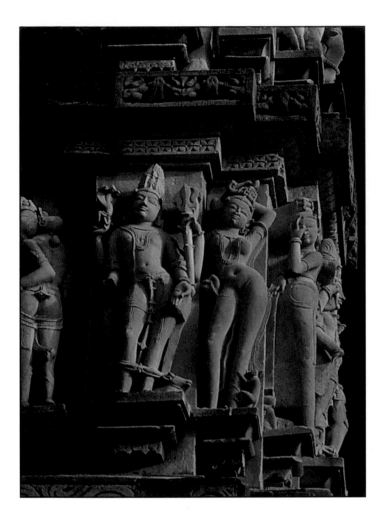

sculptors preferred to let the human drama unfold itself without the benefit of a natural setting, so that the principal characters are highlighted. Floral and geometrical motifs are decorative in nature and are not true to detail, the artist using them only for purposes of design and often exaggerating details.

Above left: *The north-facing lower band of Kandariya Mahadev Temple has this study of an apsara disrobing while a monkey pulls at her saree. The main subject, that of a woman undressing, has been profusely depicted at Khajuraho.*

Above right: *An image of Vishnu framed within a bracket in the right subsidiary shrine of Lakshman Temple.*

Why Erotics?

The profusion of erotic sculptures at Khajuraho is confusing; do they represent the lax morals of a decadent society, are they an aid to sex education, or do they point the way from the base, i.e. lust, to the sublime? Are they an attempt to procure salvation for the mythical Hemvati, or are they intended to ward off evil spirits? If the latter, they have certainly succeeded in keeping the legacy of the temples alive over a thousand years, despite their being isolated for centuries. These sculptures are from the north-facing middle and upper bands of Vishvanath Temple.

Top left and right: *Sculptures of Lakshmi-Narayan (Vishnu with his consort Lakshmi) suggest benevolence and generosity of spirit. These images are from the south-facing lower bands of Parsvanath Temple.*

IF THE EROTIC COMPONENT OF KHAJURAHO'S temple sculptures invites comment, it is with good reason. Perhaps no other collection of medieval art uses the body-metaphor as voluptuously as these sculptures. The temple walls are a living, seething mass of life and vitality; celebrating youth and beauty, they are the sanctuary of lovers, both divine and human. Unabashed, incredibly frank, the erotic quality of Khajuraho is disturbing, but also cleansing: this is the love sanctioned by the gods, a love unaccompanied by guilt and one which knows only the language of pleasure.

Sexual intercourse forms only one component of Khajuraho's sculptural art; the Jain or Vishnu tem-ples, for instance, possess little or no eroticism, and the scenes represented on the Shiva temples as often depict everyday life as sexual union. But it is in designing the lines of the human body that the erotic prevails. The female form is profusely depicted, with round breasts and generous curves, twisting and turning in sinuous poses, each movement recorded in the minutest detail. Men wage war or sit in conference, or provide the male component of a couple; they are depicted with all their blemishes— pot-bellied, lecherous, willing to rest, to watch—the prop for the more energetic female form who, crafted over and over, in varying moods, nevertheless emerges as a mysterious figure, one that men cannot fully understand.

Most visitors are surprised to discover that the much-publicised erotic scenes form only a small part of Khajuraho's sculptural wealth; yet, in the file of Khajuraho memories, it is always the erotic factor which remains associated with the temples. Does it mirror the ultimate decadence of a depraved society, or explain the profound philosophy of a highly enlightened one?

Explanations have been sought at various times by various people, from scholars like Mulk Raj Anand, Vidya Prakash and Kanwarlal to the local guides and gurus. The simplest explanation reverts to the legend of Hemvati and her brief, passionate interlude with the Moon god, which could only be condoned through the performance of the ritual *bhandya-yagya* by her emperor-son. The ritual of the *yagya* included the depiction of erotic figures or pictures *(bhandya-chitra)* as admissions of guilt and as lessons in morality. Is it not possible that, once Hemvati's guilt had been absolved, rulers of the dynasty went back to the same images in successive temples, both to remind the people of how the dynasty began, and to continually propitiate the gods?

Carvings of couples performing the sexual act, known as *mithuns*, are routinely depicted on temples, since the Indian *shastras* (canons) consider them propitious symbols that ward off evil and render the building immune to destruction. Historically, *mithun* sculptures, motifs or symbols have been depicted in India over a period of nearly 2,000 years, from the 2nd century BC to at least the 17th century AD. They are present at the shrines of various religious sects in the whole geographical vastness of India, from Kashmir to Kerala and from Gujarat to Assam. Some scholars suggest that the artist in Khajuraho simply followed the general tradition, carving the *mithuns* as a matter of course; if this is so, he took

This panel from the north wall of Lakshman Temple has a bevy of outstanding sculptures. These include this mithun couple with attendants depicting foreplay. While figures in horizontal panels are placed without any sense of predetermined order, vertically the subjects ascend from battles and scenes of everyday life to celestial beings, culminating in images of deities.

This page: *A wild abandonment in body movement combines with containment in self expression as this couple gaze with tenderness into each other's eyes while they make love. To their left, the apsara pressing her bosom expresses her own arousal.*

Facing page: *The apsara discards her lower garments; the scorpion on her thigh denotes passion. Note the details of the lower abdomen, the wrinkles on the pubic area: since the bosom is held high, the wrinkles are evidently not the result of old age, but are perhaps caused by childbirth. This sculpture is from the lower band that faces north (the sculpture faces east) of Devi Jagdamba Temple .*

considerable license with their depiction, for their sheer number is overwhelming; nor does this explanation provide an answer to the question: why has the woman been so sensuously carved as the focal point of the temples?

It is possible that the earlier beliefs which attached no stigma to sex found expression on the temple walls to correct the erroneous thinking of preachers, including the Buddha himself, who chose to forget the fundamental ingredient of being. Buddha in his wisdom wished to banish woman, love, sex and beauty from the life of man. As a result, the pendulum later swung to the extreme, as we discover in several Buddhist and Hindu creeds prevalent at the time when the temples of Khajuraho were constructed; not only in India, but also in Nepal, Tibet, China and several other lands. The pleasures granted by centuries of Hindu thought and philosophy, which the Buddha had banished, were revived; frugality and abstinence were rejected in favour of self-expression and sensuality sanctioned by religion. And what better way to proclaim the revival

A lesson in sex education? This panel from a lower, south-facing band of Vishvanath Temple is placed below the larger sculptures. It would appear that a teacher is imparting the theory of sex from an open book before him; one of the pupils is overcome with shyness while witnessing the live demonstration concurrent to the teaching.

than by the depiction of women, love and pleasure on the walls of temples?

The temples of Khajuraho, with their contemporaries in Gujarat, Rajasthan and Orissa, also mirror certain social and philosophical attitudes of the age. For man, life has always posed a choice between acceptance of the body at the cost of the soul, and denial of the flesh for the sake of the spirit. But every now and then, as in the golden, prosperous age of the Chandelas, men seem to have reconciled the physical and the spiritual, proving that mind and matter need not necessarily be at war. To enjoy the delights of *arth* (material wealth) and *kama* (sensual pleasures) while performing one's *dharma* (duty) was the accepted way of life for the *grihastha* (householder). The complete scheme of life included these essential stages on the path to detachment so that, when ripe for the next stage of *moksha* (liberation), man could renounce both without reluctance or regret. The temple structure is also seen in these stages. The *ardh-mandap* is allegorised as *dharma*, the *mandap* as *arth*, the *antaral* as *kama* (this portion contains most of the erotic sculptures) and the *garbh-griha* signifying the liberation of *moksha*.

During ancient and medieval periods in India, education was imparted by Brahmins or priests within temple precincts, and there were fully developed treatises on all subjects including sex. Thus, as the most popular place of assembly and education, the temple itself became a storehouse of knowledge, with a language of its own; its walls carried lessons in philosophy, religion, mythology, codes of conduct and social behaviour, as well as sexual hygiene and morality. Against this backdrop, the *mithun* sculptures can be seen as merely imparting sex education and ingraining in students the realization of the sensual life as an essential step on the journey from householder to renunciator.

Healthy copulation is shown to open the doors to earthly bliss, as is evident from the look of contentment on the faces of amorous couples; intercourse with beasts, on the other hand, becomes the door to hell; mark the expressions of those indulging in bestial, unnatural practices. The placement of the two, one much higher and the other at a low level, accentuates this teaching.

Life presents a constant struggle between the physical and the spiritual; according to Hindu thought the conflict can only be resolved through discipline and self-control. Hence, one reaches the purity of the sanctum only after reflecting on, and leaving behind, the attractions of the senses. To highlight this, the erotics are placed mainly on the exterior walls; when they appear inside a temple, it is on the ambulatory, the path around the sanctum — thus becoming the ultimate test of one's resolution.

Yoga is an ancient discipline in India and the erotics are considered by some to be demonstrations of exercises which combine yoga with sex. According to yogic belief, what can cause destruction in the hands of the ignorant and the foolish can be transformed into an instrument of the highest good by the wise. So also with the fire of lust, which the yogi converts, through psycho-physical controls and exercises, into luminiscence and energy of amazing power and degree.

Pragmatists draw attention to the fact that the temple served as the socio-religious centre of the community. A large number of pilgrims helped to fill the state coffers; the *mithun* carvings, like the *devdasis* (temple-

This page: *These figures, placed between elephants in a frieze from Lakshman Temple, depict the start of sexual intimacy between a couple. The man has slipped his fingers into the woman's garments to kindle her energy force, which will arrive at its natural culmination—the fusion of energy through intercourse.*

Overleaf: *Two bands of sculpture from the south wall of Lakshman Temple. The central figures in the lower band depict a well-known erotic couple; the adjacent attendants are seen stimulating themselves with auto-eroticism.*

This scene of erotic congress is characteristic of tantrism with the male and female forms aligned with the north and south poles, the union being assisted by female attendants in a perfect concentration of consciousness and energy.

Tantrism

TANTRISM AS A HINDU PHILOSOPHY enjoyed a large following from approximately the eighth to the fourteenth centuries, with the medieval ages being the period when it reached its peak. A religious system based on Hindu thought, it was complicated in its rituals, although it promised what amounted to the quickest form of *moksha* or liberation from the cycle of rebirths.

At its simplest level Tantrism, like Hinduism, believes that the entire universe undergoes a constant process of creation, preservation and transformation. At the fulcrum of this are consciousness and energy, the first a male principle, the second, female. The union of the two is the basis of creation, preservation and transformation, for nature is never static but in a state of flux.

In the human world, sexual intercourse is a binding of the negative and positive forces of creation, and correlates with the natural world. This theory found wide acceptance in medieval India with the nobility of the period and was practised as a cult, with temples lending it their support. For the first time, therefore, erotic images were openly and profusely placed on temple façades.

The complete melding of the principles of consciousness and energy are to be seen in those erotic sculptures in which the two halves of a couple appear to be part of each other, in total cohesion, the man's eyes often trance-like, indicating that the being is in harmony with the Absolute.

The temples themselves, with their flow and changing images at different times of day, lend support to the theory of tantrism being practised at Khajuraho. Some feel that even the geometric design of the temples depicts the rekindling of energy forces. Tantra itself has its root in the Sanskrit word for body, and implies the feeling of the cosmos within the body: that is, all the energy forces present in nature, in concentrated form, can be found within the body, thus providing the shortest way to salvation. A perfect example of tantric intercourse is the yogic sexual posture on the façade of Kandariya Mahadev Temple which shows the male standing on his head, the female mounted above, their bodies perfectly aligned with the north and south pole, in a fusion of the energies of the cosmos.

dancers), were a means of attracting them. At the same time, in view of the competition faced from other sects and religions, it was religious allegory in the form of erotic art that acted as a means of defense: voyeurs, and others who came to scoff, so the theory went, would eventually remain to pray. This theory might not be as simplistic as it appears when one realises that, even a thousand years later, they serve as the initial draw for many visitors who, likewise, return onriched and enlightened.

Some observers suggest that the erotic sculptures illustrate the rites and practices of comparitively obscure religious cults — Tantriks, Shakts, Kauls and Kapaliks, sexual union being one of the essentials in their ceremonial worship. Apparently these sects were in existence during the period of the Khajuraho temples and had their centres in the region surrounding the Chandela kingdom. Also in the area were several tribal belts, and the influence of their fertility cults cannot be ruled out.

Finally, there are the interpretations of ancient and profound philosophies which find expression on the temple walls. According to the Hindu story of creation,

This is a typical erotic posture from Khajuraho, depicted on the upper band of the north wall of Vishvanath temple. The posture is based on yogic exercise, that of the sheerasana or the head posture, with the woman upside down. Two female assistants support the couple, with the woman's fingers fondling the genitalia of one of them. At best this is an imaginary posture. Mithun exercises of this nature also have some basis in the spread of tantrism prevalent at the time in the region, with sexual union used as a shortcut to gaining moksha or liberation from the chain of rebirths.

the *Adidev* (God in the beginning) was neither male nor female. Overcome by loneliness, it divided itself into two equal halves—*purush* (man) and *nari* (woman)—so that each remained incomp-lete without the other. Only as a result of the union of these halves could the world enjoy fertility. A couple is seen as a symbol of the duality of god and nature, of opposites such as light and darkness, and even as *atma* (soul) and *paramatma* (divine); their coming together signifies the essential unity of the universe.

Carving religion and philosophy on their temple walls in such a harmonious manner as to unite sculpture with architecture, the legacy of the Chandelas eventually appears to be one of a perfect balance between the physical and the spiritual. But, as with all great works of art, the ultimate interpretation lies within each individual, at a personal level of understanding and appreciation. The temples of Khajuraho symbolise a profound philosophy for those who would justify it; degradation for those who condemn it.

Pages 64-65: *This panel from the outer side of the platform of Lakshman Temple, facing south-east, is part of a running frieze depicting scenes from a battlefield.*

Facing page: *Much of the sensuousness in the sculptures in Khajuraho is to be found in the delicate grace with which the figures of women, such as this dancer, have been crafted.*

This page: *In this mithun from the north-facing middle band of Vishvanath Temple the helper shyly hides her face as the man penetrates his lover from behind. In this position she appears to be bending in supplication before an ascetic who, in turn, is stimulating himself.*

Architecture

The 85 temples built between the 9th and 12th centuries were governed by a common architectural style. This picture sis of the ceiling of the entrance porch of Lakshman Temple, rated by many as among the best in the country for its exquisite carving. This is the only example of a with all four subsidiary shrines intact.

69

The vertical movement of the temple façades is arrested by the placement of balconies and windows, though, viewed from a distance, they too aid the overall composition by blending with the upward flow while providing light and air to the inner walls and ambulatories. This picture shows the portico with its windows overlooking the sculptures of the south wall of Devi Jagdamba Temple.

WHEN THE GREEK INVASIONS TOOK PLACE IN THE 3rd century BC, temple worship did not exist in India. Hinduism was more philosophical than ritualistic in its outlook and practice. The institution of the temple as a place of worship was largely due to the rise of Buddhism; the Buddhists placed symbolic representations of their founder in their stupas, and between the 2nd and 7th centuries the Buddhist upsurge was so powerful that it seemed Buddhism might become the national religion. This it failed to do because the shrewd Hindu Brahmin priests sensed the situation and set about matching Buddhist myth and ritual with even more fanciful flights of theological thought and festive forms of worship.

It was during this process of reorientation that the institution of the temple was seriously taken over by Hinduism. Adding grandeur and grace to the shape of the temple, ornamentation and decoration to its entire structure and significance to the ritual of worship, the Hindus achieved wonders in just a few centuries of temple building. The temples of Khajuraho depict this activity at its zenith and, in the 'nagara' (Indo-Aryan) category to which they belong, they mark the point of perfection. No part is superfluous or out of place, whether from the point of view of the most exacting architectural standards or of the most elaborate religious symbolism.

Of the 85 temples believed to have been built by the Chandela kings, 20 remain in various stages of preserva-tion. The existence of nearly 50 other shrines is traceable in ruins scattered extensively over the area. There are three groups of temples at Khajuraho, based on their location. The large Western Group consists of the Chausath Yogini, Lalguan Mahadev, Parvati, Varaha, Matangeshwar, Lakshman, Vishvanath, Nandi, Chitragupta, Devi Jagdamba and Kandariya Mahadev. The seven temples of the Eastern Group include four Jain temples—Parsvanath, Adinath, Shantinath and Ghantai—and three Brahmanical ones—Vamana, Javari and Brahma. This is also known as the Jain group. The small Southern Group contains the Chaturbhuj and Duladeo temples. The Kandariya Mahadev is considered the most evolved example of central Indian temple architecture.

The Khajuraho temples are not affiliated to any one sect or religion. There are temples dedicated to Shiva, Vishnu and the Jain Tirthankaras, but in architectural style and composition there is nothing to distinguish a Jain temple from a Shiva or Vishnu temple. Often there is no connec-tion between the name of a temple and the deity installed within; due to theft or destruction of the original deity, a replacement was often installed at a later date. The Brahma temple housing Shiva and the Devi Jagdamba temple with the goddess Parvati in its sanctum were both originally dedicated to Vishnu. This is evident from the prominence given to Vishnu on the sanctum doorway. Similarly, the Parsvanath temple was earlier dedicated to Adinath; originally it was probably a Hindu temple, going by its lavish portrayal of the Hindu pantheon.

The simile of the Himalayan mountains or Mount Kailash (the mythical abode of Lord Shiva) is often used in the construction of the temples. The Chandela inscriptions describe the temple spires as 'rivals of the peaks of mountains of snow'. From the frontal perspective, the temple entrance is dark and cave-like in appearance. The name of Khajuraho's largest temple, the Kandariya Mahadev, translates to mean 'the great Lord who resides in a mountain cave', i.e.

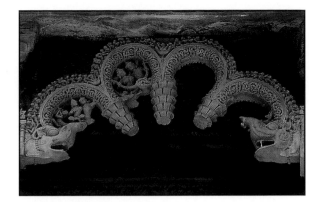

This page: *The torana is an important architectural embellishment to the entrance of a temple. Buddhist stupas had toranas decorated with figures, but were more severe in design than the Hindu temple torana, which probably derived from its Buddhist source. This four-loop torana at the entrance to Kandariya Mahadev Temple is carved from a single stone and the richly sculptured loops with their gandharvas and kinnaras culminate on the heads of mythical crocodiles.*

Pages 72-73: *The entrance to the sanctum of Devi Jagdamba Temple is profusely sculptured, though the main figures on either side have been defaced. The lintel above shows that the temple was originally dedicated to Vishnu, though the image within the sanctum is now that of Parvati.*

South elevation, Vishvanath temple. This temple is typical of the Khajuraho style: built on a platform it shares with a Nandi shrine, it has an ardh-mandap, a mandap, a maha-mandap, an antaral and a garba griha with an ambulatory. Its outer façade has the traditional three bands of sculpture.

Lord Shiva. All the temples have one entrance and most of them face east, with the excep-tion of the Chaturbhuj and the Lalguan Mahadev temples which face west and the Chausath Yogini, facing north.

The ground plan of the Khajuraho temples has four compartments—the *ardh-mandap* or entrance porch; the *mandap*, an assembly hall; the *antaral* or vestibule and the *garba-griha* or sanctum, where the deity is installed. The *mandap*, while imparting elegance, also served as the waiting hall for the devotees, and provided them with shelter from the rain or heat. In some temples an extra *mandap*—the *maha mandap*—is added for size and splendour; it is distinguished from the *mandap* by its pair of lateral transepts. Some of the larger temples have an inner ambulatory (*pradakshina*) around the sanctum, in which case the sanctum also has a pair of lateral transepts and a rear transept. Technically, temples with one pair of lateral transepts are called *nirandhar* and those with two pairs *sandhar*.

The ceiling of each compartment is supported on

74

beams and architraves, resting on walls, pillars and pilasters. The minor compartments normally have flat ceilings relieved by the lotus design. The larger ceiling of the *maha mandap* is carried on a square framework of architraves supported on four central pillars. This square framework graduates into an octagonal shape before turning circular at the top. The floor of each succeeding compartment of the temple is on a higher level so that the last, the *garba-griha*, is placed at the highest level.

This vertical move or upward pull is evident everywhere, beginning with the solid masonry of the *jagati*. This, the open, spacious platform on which each temple stands, is a distinguishing feature of Khajuraho temples. The Lakshman temple, with which the Khajuraho style takes on a distinct identity, still has its original platform intact. The elevation plan of the temples consists of the basement storey — the *adisthana* — on the *jagati*, over which rests the *jangha* or the wall portion of the temple, forming the central zone. The balconied openings set in these walls form another striking feature of the Khajuraho temples. While they make a picturesque contrast of voids and solids, they also serve to admit air and light into the shrine. Above the *jangha* is the *shikhar* or the spire. Each compartment has its individual roof; just as the floors within the temples are set at successively higher levels, so the corresponding roofs outside rise in tiers.

Each roof is covered with a cluster of *shikhars* and *uru-shikhars* (half-spires) arranged in a rise-and-break design, with a maximum congregation on the roof over the sanctum. The curvilinear *shikhars* are crowned by an *amalak* and a *kalash* which together form a distinctive feature of the 'nagara' temples. The *kalash*—the water pot or auspicious jar—is the container of nectar, the prize to which the devotee aspires, his release from the world of death and decay. The *amalak*, a ribbed ring of stone, encircles the *kalash* and denotes pure essence.

The temple is often seen as a human body housing God in its soul (sanctum). The base or the *adisthana* represents legs, the mid-portion *jangha* is seen as the waist, and the top, the *shikhar*, becomes the head with its crown of *kalash* and *amalak*. Some of the larger temples have subsidiary shrines on each corner of the *jagati*, making the structure a complete *panchayatan* (complex of five shrines). Although the Kandariya

This page: *The hanging bell column from Ghantai Temple has sculptures of gandharvas, kinnaras and vidyadhars (floating celestial beings).*

Overleaf: *A full view of Lakshman Temple with Matangeshwar to one side. Lakshman Temple is important, for it is the only surviving temple in Khajuraho built in the north Indian panchayatana style with a main shrine and four subsidiary shrines. Usually in such cases the subsidiary shrines house the family gods of the main deity from the principal sanctum. In the case of this Vishnu temple, the subsidiaries would have been dedicated to Durga, Indra, Surya and Agni, but do not house these original images any more.*

The maha-mandap of Devi Jagdamba Temple with the gateway to the inner sanctum visible. While the gateway is carved with images of divinities, the load-bearing pillars are almost totally devoid of ornamentation. In temples such as Lakshman or Kandariya Mahadev these pillars are decorated with images of gods and goddesses, shalbhanjikas and gandharvas and usually culminate in the squat dwarf images of Keechak. All the temples had pillars on which the ceilings rested.

Mahadev and Vishvanath temples are also of the *panchayatan* type, only the Lakshman temple has all four corner shrines intact.

The gradual evolution of the Khajuraho temple over two centuries can be seen from the simple granite Chausath Yogini and the Brahma temples through the Matangeshwar, Lakshman, Vishvanath and the Kandariya Mahadev, and finally the Chatur-bhuj and Duladeo. Made of coarse-grained granite, the tiny shrines of the Chausath Yogini have elemen-tary *shikhars* and no ornamentation. The Brahma and the Lalguan Mahadev exhibit the transition in the building material used with their granite bodies and roofs of sandstone. In the Varaha, granite remains limited to the lower half of the plinth and the Matangeshwar becomes the first temple built wholly of sandstone. The balconied windows, elementary cusps in the ceiling and some ornamentation has started taking shape in these temples, but the Khajuraho style actually comes into its own with the Lakshman temple. With this temple begins the ascent which progresses in

the Parsvanath, Vishvanath, Devi Jagdamba and Chitragupta, finally reaching its peak in the unrivalled Kandariya Mahadev.

During the various stages of development, the two-loop *makar-torana* develops into a *torana* of five loops, the plain *mandap* roofs become ornamental, the flat walls give way to balconied windows and the simple *shikhar* becomes elaborate and striking with numerous subsidiary *shikhars*. The simple, single cella becomes a five-shrine complex with an ambulatory around the sanctum. The simultaneous development of sculpture is also evident as bare walls are filled with encircling bands of sculptures and processional friezes on the base, in the recessions and on the projections. There is no further evolution beyond the Kandariya Mahadev. The Vaman, Adinath and Javari are smaller in scale but manage, nevertheless, to maintain the same style. The decline in the art of Khajuraho sets in with the Chaturbhuj and Duladeo temples which exhibit undue and monotonous emphasis on ornamentation.

This page: *The circumambulatory passage around the sanctum of Lakshman Temple has a number of very good sculptures that reveal the depth into which the sculpture was carved in the round. At right is Gajalakshmi, Vishnu's consort, while the figure with the beard is that of Agni, the God of Fire. Interspersed among these divinities are celestial nymphs in a number of postures.*

Overleaf: *A view of Duladeo Temple from the back, with the restoration work done on the spires clearly visible. Dedicated to Shiva, it has a shikhar surrounded by three minor shikhars and an unusually long ardh-mandap leading into an octagonal maha-mandap.*

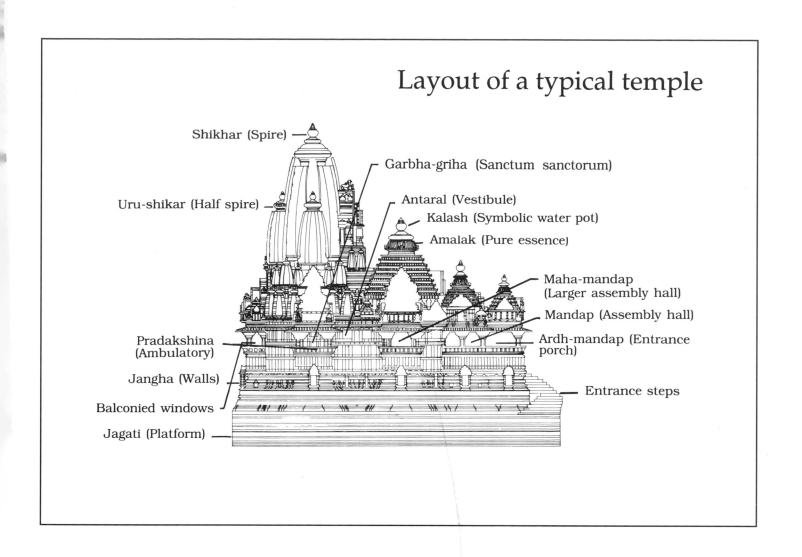

Layout of a typical temple

Shikhar (Spire)

Uru-shikar (Half spire)

Garbha-griha (Sanctum sanctorum)

Antaral (Vestibule)

Kalash (Symbolic water pot)

Amalak (Pure essence)

Maha-mandap (Larger assembly hall)

Mandap (Assembly hall)

Pradakshina (Ambulatory)

Ardh-mandap (Entrance porch)

Jangha (Walls)

Balconied windows

Entrance steps

Jagati (Platform)

In comparision with its contemporaries in Orissa, Gujarat and Rajasthan, the Khajuraho temple has the highly evolved *sapta-ratha* (structure with seven projections) sanctum and *saptanga-bada* (seven segments) cubical portion below the *shikhar.* The temples of Orissa generally have a five-projection sanctum with a five-segment cubical portion, while those of Gujarat have a five-projection sanctum with normally a three-segment cubical portion. In Orissa the *shikhar* over the sanctum is comparatively severe, with no subsidiary towers, and the *mandaps* are plain. The different compartments of the Khajuraho temple form a compact and integrated complex, as opposed to the the inordinately long halls of the Orissa temple. The earliest *sandhar* temples of Rajasthan bear close resemblance to those of Khajuraho, with a similar architectural plan and design, but lack the *apsara* brackets and the sculptural profusion.

Outline of a typical Khajuraho temple, each part leading from the one before it to become a cohesive whole, symbolic with the human body and indicative of the ascent to heaven.

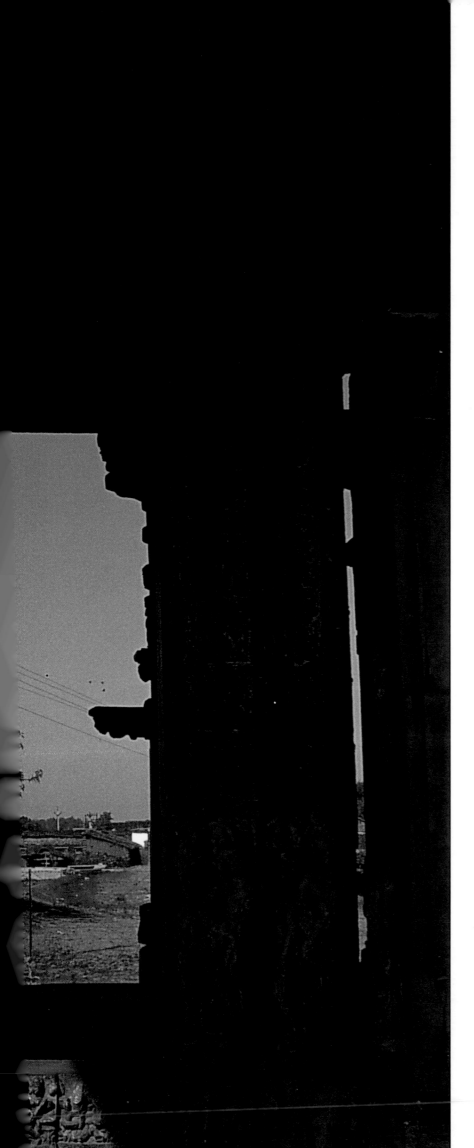

Oblivion and Rediscovery

Time took its toll on the temples, a thousand years old, especially since they were abandoned. This picture depicts the village of Khajuraho as framed within the ruins of Ghantai Temple. The temple is known for its pillars decorated with motifs of hanging bells from which it takes its name.

A modern shrine dedicated to Hanuman, the monkey god associated with Lord Ram, hero of the epic Ramayana, located en route to the village of Khajuraho. The image is regularly layered with a paste of sandalwood, turmeric and vermilion; devotees flick off the paste to place on their foreheads while seeking the blessings of the gods.

THE DWINDLING POWER OF THE CHANDELA RAJPUTS had shrunk their realm, and by the 12th and 13th centuries their limited capital was of little political interest. Alternate power centres developed, and the once-wealthy feudatory empire could no longer extend its patronage to the arts; in consequence, the settlements grew smaller as artisans looked to other states for their livelihood.

Where once there were the vestiges of an empire, the forest now encroached, swamping buildings, tanks and temples. The dark canopy of the forest lent sanctuary to wild beasts; but through the under-growth, along paths they knew, people from nearby settlements, whose ancestors had worshipped at the shrines of the Chandelas, journeyed on special occasions to pray before Shiva.

The lost temples of Khajuraho were rediscovered in the 19th century, but would have to wait till well into the 20th century before they could regain the fame they enjoyed during the reign of the Chandelas. The intervening years provided only the occasional passing

reference from a traveller chronicling his journey.

With the decline of the Chandela dynasty after Vidyadhar (1018-1029 AD), Khajuraho was known only as a minor religious centre; it was accorded none of the importance given to Hindu pilgrimage spots such as Banaras. Most of its temples were abandoned; the only one still used for worship was the Matangeshwar with its large Shivling. The rest were just stones and ruins harbouring wildlife and sometimes ascetics. This is attested by Ibn-Batuta, who visited Khajuraho in 1335; he calls it 'Kajarra'—'where there is a great pond about a mile in length near which are temples containing idols which the Muslims have mutilated. In the centre of that pond there are three cupolas of red stone, each of three storeys; and at the far corner of the pond are cupolas in which live a body of the jogis who have clotted their hair and let them grow so that they become as long as their bodies and on account of their practising asceticism their colour had become extremely yellow. Many Musalmans follow them in order to take lessons from them. It is said that

Padam Chandel is known as Matang Baba and has lived at the foot of Matangeshwar Temple for as long as anyone can remember. Though he does not visit the Shiva temple, and often raises his voice in anger against the gods, he spends much of his time sweeping the path to the temple. Guides sometimes refer to this ascetic with his matted hair as a member of the Chandela dynasty, but the veracity of this claim has never been established.

whoever is subjected to diseases like leprosy or elephantisis lives with them for a long period of time and is cured by the permission of God.'

Sikander Lodi reached the tract in 1495; fortunately he was just passing through, and lacked sufficient men and time to cause as much destruction as he might have desired. By the 16th century Khajuraho was such an insignificant little village that it did not even merit a mention in the *Ain-i-Akbari,* Abul Fazl's chronicle of the Mughal court.

The credit for rediscovering the temples of Khajuraho belongs to T. S. Burt, a British engineer, who traversed the region in 1838. He wrote in his journal: 'Some of the sculptures here are extremely indecent and offensive, which I was at first much surprised to find in temples....'. Alexander Cunningham made a detailed survey between 1852 and 1885 and in his Archaeological Survey Reports (Volumes II, VII, X and XXI, issued between 1871 and 1885) dwelt upon inscriptions, mounds and images found scattered in the area.

A thousand years ago this primitive hamlet,

Facing page: Devotees bathe in the waters of Sivsagar Lake close to the Western Group of temples before praying at Matangeshwar Temple during Shivratri. At other times ritual bathing in the water tank is not allowed, and visitors can opt for a boat ride.

This page: A sadhu collects offerings made to Ganesh, the elephant-headed god who is propitiated as the remover of obstacles. This Ganesh image is seated on the platform of Matangeshwar Temple, and offerings of coins and flowers are often placed before the deity.

Though Hindu, the temples of Khajuraho may well have a lesson that is secular and appeals to a wide cross-section of visitors. Here, nuns stand on the platform of a well in the Western Group as they survey Vishvanath and Parvati temples.

surrounded by inhospitable terrain, was a thriving city; by the first half of the 20th century it was just one of the millions of villages dotting the Indian countryside, only its group of temples setting it apart from the rest. Even nature had changed; gone were the *khajurs* from which the city derived its name, replaced by mahua trees whose golden flowers turned into intoxicant fruit, used to brew country liquor.

It was only after the visit of India's first President, Dr. Rajendra Prasad, to Khajuraho in 1953 that the Archaeological Survey of India took up the task of clearing, fencing and restoring the temples. Then their potential was finally realised; they were hailed as the find of the century, as important as the Ajanta and Ellora caves. With only a small Circuit House, also built in 1953, Khajuraho now attracted art historians, scholars and offbeat travellers whose intensity of purpose saw them through tedious journeys over rough terrain.

Two such travellers were Shyam Poddar and his companion, Bert Hemphill. The year was 1955 and the travellers were struck by the place's immense potential as a tourist destination. But how was it to be displayed on the tourism map of the world? Khajuraho was 32 miles from the nearest town; 62 miles from a railway station; no flights came even close to it.

In January 1966, the foundation stone of Khajuraho's first modern hotel was laid in the presence of 105 members of the international travel trade attending a conference in Delhi. Their arrival made history; five aircraft landed here for the first time on a freshly-made fair-weather airstrip. One can imagine the bewilderment of the villagers who saw these *cheel-gaadi* (bird-cars) as they landed, and out of whose bellies emerged strange men and women with golden, yellow and even red hair. The delegates, meanwhile, recieved their first taste of Khajuraho's backwardness as they tried to disembark —in the absence of an airport there was no step-ladder, and a makeshift one had to be procured from the construction site of the hotel.

The struggle had just begun—for an air-service, better roads, water, telephones and other basic facilities required of a tourist resort. Statistically, the village of Khajuraho was a poor contender for these *vis-a-vis* other towns, but Shyam Poddar's enthusiasm ensured that the resurrection got underway.

Today Khajuraho has luxury hotels, a modern runway and airport, shops, banking and communication facilities, swimming pools and health clubs, air-conditioned restaurants and car-hire companies. This is one Indian village where signs are posted in three foreign languages; its temples have been declared 'World Heritage' monuments by the United Nations.

With Khajuraho becoming increasingly popular, the potential of its rich surroundings is also unfolding. The Panna diamond mines, Rajgarh Palace and the Pandav and Raneh Falls form easy excursions out of Khajuraho. A little further, the ancient fortress of Kalinjar and the beautiful monuments of Orchha are also coming into the limelight. The jungle which once overgrew the temples has receded a few kilometres to form the Panna National Park, a wildlife sanctuary.

The river goddess Ganga (top) and a dwarf with a container of nectar (above). The rivers Ganga and Yamuna are considered sacred by Hindus and are usually placed at the entrance to the temple. These sculptures are from the Museum.

89

Dance Festival

The annual dance festival at Khajuraho brings together the best of the country's talent to perform against the exciting backdrop of the temples.

FOR A WEEK IN MARCH EVERY YEAR, the Western Group of temples becomes the setting for a dance festival. The event, now on the international calendar, though the dance forms are classical Indian, is organised by the cultural department of Madhya Pradesh.

The Vishvanath Temple is used as the floodlit background for the event, staged after sunset. Participation is limited to dancers with creditable reputations, and includes names that have burned bright on the artistic firmament for years.

It can be safely surmised that the use of the temples as a stage depicting Indian classical dances—ranging from Bharatanatyam and Kathak to Odissi, Chhau, Kuchipudi, Kathakali and Manipuri, among others — is a contemporary happening. Sculptures on the temple walls depict dancers in poses from folk-art forms that were native to the region; it is possible that some of these dances were also staged within the temples. These are not now known, and such dance forms — any folk dance forms, in fact — have not been used at the festival.

The musical instruments depicted on the sculptures are, however, still in use, many being employed during the festival (although music only plays a functional role here, in support of the dances, which are the real highlight of the festival).

90

The Temples: A Guide

ADINATH

(11th century AD; Eastern Group)

Dedication: Jain (modern image of Adinath).

Architectural features: Similar to Vamana in plan; *shikhar* is lighter and more proportionate. Only *antaral* and *garba griha* without ambulatory remain (*ardh-mandap* and *mandap* destroyed).

Sculptural specialities: Beautiful lattice work patterns of *chaitya* windows along its sides. Three bands of sculptural decorations depicting celestial beauties and deities. Topmost band is smaller than lower two and carries figures of apsaras, attendants with garlands and musical instruments. Of particular note: the band of flying *vidyadhars* (a class of celestial beings). Roof of *antaral* has beautiful carvings.

BRAHMA

(c. 925 AD; Eastern group)

Dedication: Shiva (earlier dedicated to Vishnu).

Architectural features: Granite body, *shikhar* of sandstone. Simple structure with a porch and a sanctum. Pyramidal roof with receding tiers.

Sculptural specialities: Latticed windows. Four-faced linga in sanctum. Plain doorway except for figures of river goddesses Ganga and Yamuna on either side of doorway and base; trinity of Brahma, Vishnu and Shiva on lintel.

CHATURBHUJ

(c. 1100 AD; Southern Group)

Dedication: Shiva.

Architectural features: High platform. Faces west. Highly compressed *ardh-mandap, mandap,* constricted *antaral* and *garbha griha* without ambulatory. Heavy and simple *shikhar* with curvilinear shape but no spires or turrets.

Sculptural specialities: Absence of erotic sculptures. Three bands of sculptural panels on exterior, including Narsinghi (consort of Narsingh—only such sculpture in India) and Ardhnarishwar (half-male, half-female representation of divinity). Remarkable four-armed Dakshinmurti Shiva in sanctum; largest sanctum idol at Khajuraho. Facial expression reveals Buddhist influence. Rare manifestation of Shiva as Supreme Teacher — some scholars think it is Vishnu.

CHAUSATH YOGINI

(c. 850 AD; Western Group)

Dedication: Shakti (64 yoginis which represent different aspects of Shakti)

Architectural Features: Coarse-grained granite structure. 64 cells in quadrangular plan with a courtyard. Facing north.

Structural specialities: Surviving images in sandstone— *Mahishasurmardini* (central shrine); Maheshwari and Brahmani (flanking shrines).

CHITRAGUPTA

(c. 1000 AD; Western Group)

Dedication: Surya (sun god).

Architectural features: Fairly well preserved, except for porch which has been renovated. Octagonal ceiling. *Ardh-mandap, maha-mandap* with lateral transepts, *antaral, garbha griha* without ambulatory.

Sculptural specialities: Carvings on basement show dancing and hunting sce-nes, warriors, elephants and cavaliers in procession and stone carvers. Impressive image of Surya in sanctum. Shown riding his chariot with seven horses representing days of the week.

DEVI JAGDAMBA

(c. 1000 AD; Western Group)

Dedication: Parvati (spouse of Shiva); originally

dedicated to Vishnu.

Architectural features: Common plinth with Kandariya Mahadev. *Ardh-mandap, maha-mandap* with transepts; *antaral, garbha griha* without ambulatory. Balconies of hall bigger than those of other temples; roofs over them supported by five columns.

Sculptural specialities: Three bands of sculptures with divinities, celestial nymphs, erotic figures, elegant figures of women undressing and anointing themselves, lovers embracing and deities. Sanctum has crude image of Parvati (also called Kali), painted black.

DULADEO

(c. 1100-25 AD; Southern Group)

Dedication: Shiva (originally dedicated to Kartikeya, leader of the divine army).

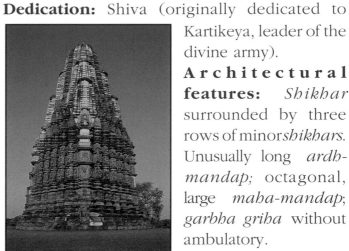

Architectural features: *Shikhar* surrounded by three rows of minor *shikhars*. Unusually long *ardh-mandap;* octagonal, large *maha-mandap*; *garbha griha* without ambulatory.

Sculptural specialities: Assembly hall has corbelled ceilings and *apsara* brackets. Figure sculptures are extremely ornate. Plastic and iconographic monotony and decadence. *Apsara* holding intricate waist ornament on outer wall and seven mother goddesses in dancing poses at entrance of sanctum are noteworthy.

GHANTAI

(End-tenth century AD; Eastern Group)

Dedication: Jain.

Architectural specialities: Similar to Parsvanath in design. Entrance hall and assembly hall survive on pillars. Flat ceiling.

Sculptural specialities: Pillars decorated with bell and chain motifs. Ornate ceiling. Doorway carved with 16 dreams of Jina Mahavir's mother.

JAVARI

(c. 1075-1100 AD; Eastern Group)

Dedication: Vishnu.

Architectural specialities: Small, with superb architectural design. *Ardh-mandap, mandap,* inconspicuous *antaral, garbha griha* without ambulatory. Projecting cornice with curved outline separates main body of temple from *shikhar.*

Sculptural specialities: Entrance porch flanked by exquisitely carved crocodiles. Exterior walls have three bands of sculptures containing graceful figures and celestial nymphs.

KANDARIYA MAHADEV

(c. 1025 AD; Western Group)
Dedication: Shiva (*lingam*).
Architectural features: The largest and tallest monument in Khajuraho. Common platform with Devi Jagdamba Temple and Mahadev shrine

(containing the Chandela emblem of young man grappling with lion). *Panchayatan* — but all four subsidiary shrines have disappeared. Five compartments: *ardh-mandap, mandap, maha-mandap* with lateral transepts, *antaral, garbha griha* with ambulatory and lateral transepts on sides and in the rear. Most evolved *shikhar* with 84 replicas of itself. Roof of compartments designed in the shape of a mountain peak, complete with *amalak* and *kalash*.

Sculptural specialities: Most ornamental mouldings on basement. Largest number of sculptures. Four-loop *torana* at entrance. Exterior temple wall has bold architectural mouldings and three broad bands of figurative sculptures. Erotics are clustered in two areas, north and south, in the junction between shrine and hall (vestibule). Brackets contain seven mother-goddesses. Seven-segment cella door. Elaborate doorway of sanctum has scrolls with mythical animals and nymphs and river goddesses Ganga and Yamuna at base. Intricate carvings on ceilings. Plain sanctum with marble lingam forms a sharp contrast to outer embellishments.

KHAJURAHO MUSEUM

Contains sculptures retrieved from the temples. Four galleries: Shaiva, Vaishnava, Jain, Assorted. Colossal sculpture of Dancing Ganesh at entrance.

Bhu-Varaha: Vishnu as giant boar lifting Earth, portrayed as a gentle goddess. Lakshmi-Narayan embracing; Buddha; Hari Hara; Nri-Varaha etc.

LAKSHMAN

(954 AD; Western Group).

Dedication: Vishnu (the deity is known as Ramchandra or Chaturbhuj).

Architectural features: Fine-grained sandstone. Only temple with original platform intact. *Panchayatan,* i.e. one main shrine with four subsidiary shrines. Only temple with all four subsidiary shrines intact. Each corner shrine has porch supported by two pillars and a sanctum. Main shrine has *ardh-mandap, maha-mandap, antaral* and *garbha griha* with an ambulatory and transepts on the sides and the rear. *shikhar* clustered with minor *shikhars.* Roofs on porch and hall are pyramidal.

Sculptural specialities: Processional friezes on platform contain scenes from daily life, religious myths, hunting and battle scenes, erotic motifs and bestiality, master architect with students and panel depicting Chandela rulers. Entrance porch has two-loop *makar-torana* (crocodile arch) flanked by gladiators. Exterior walls have two broad bands of sculptures of gods, goddesses, female figures and couples; brackets contain different forms of Vishnu; rare sculpture of Lord Ram on top panel; carving of *panchagni* (five fires) — only one of its kind in India. *chaitya*-arches in geometrical patterns on *shikhar.* Doorway of sanctum has rich carvings of lions, cherubs, incarnations of Vishnu, depiction of nine planets (*navgrahas*), figure of Lakshmi (spouse of Vishnu) and scene depicting the churning of the ocean. Exquisite carvings on ceilings. The *ardh-mandap* ceiling is rated one of the best in India. Roof is covered with miniature figures of *nagas* and *kalasas* (rain vases) with drooping foliage. Most ornate sanctum with three-headed (lion-man-boar) and four-armed image of Vishnu. In subsidiary shrine facing south, unusual Vishnu in *padmasana* (lotus posture) on sanctum entrance.

LALGUAN MAHADEV

(c. 900 AD; Western Group)

Dedication: Shiva (no image at present).
Architectural features: Granite body; roof of sandstone. Pyramidal. Facing west.
Sculptural specialities: Plain door-frame.

MATANGESHWAR

(c. 900-925 AD; Western Group. Only temple still used for worship)

Dedication: Shiva (lingam in sanctum).
Architectural features: Sandstone. High platform with square plan; pyramidal roof; balconied windows.
Sculptural specialities: Devoid of ornamentation — but the ceiling is formed of overlapping concentric courses. Large monolithic lingam (one of the largest in north India), of highly polished yellow sandstone — 3'8" diameter, 8'4" height — inside Gauripatta of 20'4" diameter. The lingam is a phallic symbol representing the creative power of Shiva.

NANDI

(c. 1002 AD; Western Group)

Dedication: Nandi (bull — Shiva's mount).
Architectural features: Detached pavilion forming part of Vishvanath complex. Square, on 12 pillars, enclosed by balustrade. Pyramidal roof of receding tiers. Circular ceiling.
Sculptural specialities: Steps flanked by elephants and lions. Overlapping concentric courses on ceiling. Polished, colossal monolithic image of Nandi faces his lord, Shiva, within the main temple.

PARSVANATH

(c. 954 AD; Eastern Group; also known as Dhangdev)

Dedication: Jain Parsvanath (originally Adinath — even earlier, Hindu).
Architectural features: Sandstone. Superior architectural beauty—design like Hindu temple. *Ardh-mandap, maha-mandap, antaral* and *garbha griha* — the last three being enclosed by a common ambulatory. No transepts, only a unique shrine attached to the back of the sanctum. Absence of balconied windows. Air and diffused light are admitted through screened openings which have sloping balustrades. Largest and best preserved among the Jain temples.
Sculptural Specialities: Entrance porch has ornate ceiling with five changing pendants. Central pendant is carved with floral patterns and terminates in two intertwined flying figures. Lavish portrayal of Hindu pantheon: ten-armed Chakreshwari; Parasuram; Balram-Revati; Ram-Sita; Hanuman. Jain deities are confined to the niches. Outer walls of sanctum have graceful celestial nymphs in various poses—writing a letter, extracting a thorn from the foot, painting the feet, playing musical instruments etc. Sanctum has image of Parsvanath flanked by nude male figure on left and nude female figure on right.

PARVATI

(c. 950-1000 AD; Western Group)

Dedication: Parvati (spouse of Shiva).
Architectural features: Modernised. Probably subsidiary to some other temple. Porch missing; of sanctum, only plinth remains.

95

SHANTINATH

(c. 1028 AD; Eastern Group)

Dedication: Jain (image of Adinath).
Architectural features: Extensively modernised. Oblong enclosure of shrine cells survives.

VAMANA

(c. 1050-75 AD; Eastern Group)

Dedication: Vishnu (Vamana is dwarf form).
Architectural features: High platform. *Ardh-mandap* (of which only plinth remains), *maha-mandap* with lateral transepts, *antaral, garbha griha* without ambulatory. Monospired *shikhar*, somewhat massive and squat.
Sculptural specialities: *Shikhar* with *chaitya* arches. Exterior walls have two rows of sculptures containing celestial beauties in different postures. Erotic scenes are almost absent — confined to subsidiary niches of roof pediments. In main niches of sanctum are figures of the trinity (Brahma, Vishnu, Shiva) with their consorts in upper row and several incarnations of Vishnu in lower. Within the sanctum, a figure of Buddha in earth-touching position on a wall. Main figure is of four-armed Vamana with an elaborate frame.

VARAHA

(c. 900-925 A.D; Western Group)

Dedication: Varaha (Vishnu's boar incarnation).
Architectural Features: No platform. Lower half of plinth of granite, upper of sandstone. Small pavilion type temple facing Lakshman Temple. Rectangular hall with pyramidal roof enshrines a huge statue of a boar.

Sculptural Specialities: Ceiling is decorated with a large lotus in relief, enclosed by a border of rosettes. Monolithic image of Varaha carved out of yellow sandstone, accompanied by serpent Sesha and earth-goddess. The image is decorated with 674 figures of gods and goddesses in neat rows, which include Brahma (creator), Vishnu (preserver), Shiva (destroyer), Saraswati (goddess of learning), Ganga (river), *navgrahas* (9 planets), *nagas* and *naginas* (male and female snakes) and *dipkals* (guardians of four cardinal points).

VISHVANATH

(c. 1002 AD; Western Group)

Dedication: Shiva (stone lingam — original one of stone and emeralds).
Architectural features: Shares platform with Nandi pavilion, which faces main shrine. *Panchayatan* — of four subsidiary shrines, only two remain. Main shrine has *ardh-mandap, mandap, maha-mandap* with transepts, *antaral, garba griha*, with ambulatory and transepts on the sides and in the rear.
Sculptural specialities: One subsidiary shrine contains a four-faced lingam and the other an image of Durga (Shiva's spouse). Three broad bands of sculptured figures. Ceiling has carved design of many-petalled flowers and hanging stamens. Within the temple, the main hall and passageway of shrine contain some of the loveliest sculptures. Notable sculptures: woman with fruit in one hand, parrot in the other; woman playing a flute; mother caressing child; celestial nymphs looking into a mirror or in dancing poses. Depictions of erotic art also present.